Controlled Query Evaluation in General Semantics with Incomplete Information

Inauguraldissertation
der Philosophisch-naturwissenschaftlichen Fakultät
der Universität Bern

vorgelegt von
Johannes Martin Werner
aus Deutschland

Leiter der Arbeit:
Prof. Dr. T. Studer
Institut für Informatik und angewandte Mathematik

Von der Philosophisch-naturwissenschaftlichen Fakultät angenommen.

Bern, den 23. April 2015   Der Dekan:
                                  Prof. Dr. G. Colangelo

ACKNOWLEDGEMENTS

To begin with, I want to thank Prof. Dr. T. Studer for his support, advice and guidance in preparation of and during my stay in Bern and also Prof. Dr. K. Stoffel for serving as second examiner of this thesis.

Many thanks are due to Prof. Dr. G. Jäger and all members of the Logic and Theory Group for providing an excellent work environment and stimulating discussions.

Additionally, I thank my family and friends for their support and patience.

Contents

Chapter 1

Introduction

Beginning in the past century, the possibilities to collect and use data of various kinds aggrandised dramatically. This development war accompanied by an enormous growth in computational power. The combination of both lead to a situation, where information is not only used for a single purpose that it was initially collected for, but also connected to various other information, reinterpreted and perhaps used or abused for purposes nobody could imagine. With the new possibilities of data usage, unfortunately there also arose possibilities to abuse provided information. Especially it lead to a huge loss in privacy.

Because of this development, it became insufficient to consider only data that is directly stored in a database or a direct consequence thereof. It is also necessary to protect against various other kinds of situations. For one, answers of a database, e.g. containing communication information, can lead to possible harmful believes, e.g. when a potential employer knows about contacts to a lawyer or to a (known) subject in a criminal case, this might raise suspicion and hence cause an application to fail. It turns out that possible *meta analyses* of controlled answers are even more problematic. Those can result in situations, where agents that query a protected database utilizing additional knowledge, e.g. the used method of data-protection, can infer the information, that was supposedly hidden. However, since it seems desirable to allow usage of not harmful information, the protection of knowledge should not lead to totally blocking all requests for data. Moreover, the need to protect some information from being revealed is often directly opposed by the need to be certain about some related information. For instance in healthcare it is necessary to have information about the spread of an infection and possible infection zones, but not desirable to give away any identifying data of infected people to avoid e.g. any harassment. Hence it is mandatory to simultaneously address both, the need to make as much safe information public as possible and the protection from potentially malicious usage of attainable data.

To cope with this newly recognized problem, in recent research various approaches and methods were studied and developed. One of the most successful variants in privacy protection are so called *controlled query evaluation mechanisms* that were pioneered in [Bis00] and [BW08]. The main idea is the following: The access-system of a database is equipped with a so called *censor*. This censor acts as a mediator between a querying agent and the database. Therefore separating storing information and maintaining privacy. As such, the censor has full access to the knowledge stored and implied by the database. In order to ensure privacy, the censor has

2

the abilities to distort the result before answering the query. For instance, it might chose to refuse ([SDJR83]) to answer or even to lie ([BKS95]), i.e. give an answer not matching the stored information. To maintain privacy in a consistent manner, even over multiple queries and answers, it can also be equipped with a history of answers or additional checking methods, other than plain database evaluation. The framework for controlled query evaluation has been applied for a variety of data models and control mechanisms, see for instance [BB04a, BB04b, BB07, BW08].

Another aspect of data hoarding is the failure of the *closed world assumption*, i.e. assuming not directly inferable information to be false. It was replaced by the *open world assumption*, that distinguishes between knowledge, i.e. facts that the database can decide to be either true of false, and unknowledge, i.e. statements that cannot be decided, e.g. because of insufficient data: A database containing climate information of the server-room does not know whether it rains outside or not.

Hence, in systems with Boolean *incomplete information*, the definition of the standard truth values slightly changes: The standard values t (true) and f (false) have to be read as "known to be true" and "known to be false" respectively. Additionally, a third truth value u (unknown) has to be added to describe that the statement can not be decided.

Goal of this thesis is to connect both, controlled query evaluation and incomplete knowledge, in a very wide framework. To this end, we adapt a specific approach for propositional logic presented in [BW08] to incomplete databases defined on general semantics, similar to the comparable approach in [Stu13]. Furthermore, we show that in case the underlying semantics has enough structure, databases on this semantics can essentially be treated like a propositional database.

Outline: In chapter 2 we explicitly state what is meant by the concepts of "semantics" and "incomplete evaluation" in a formal way. Also we introduce all basic notions and give an overview and motivation to privacy related definitions.

In chapter 3 we present example semantics to serve three purposes: Firstly, to allow comparison of the presented semantical definitions in widely known concrete realisations, secondly, to provide a more concise motivation on structural properties of semantics and lastly, to establish a general example setting against which all defined censors of chapter 5 can be tested.

In the following chapter 4, we show simplifications of the general semantic framework, that can be achieved in case the semantics is equipped with structural properties (e.g. a negation operator or an atomic base).

Finally, in chapter 5, we present censors, that work on all databases with general semantics. Let us point out, that a specialized version of the presented censors was presented in [SW14], in which the presented examples can also be found.

Chapter 2

Definitions

2.1 Notations

In this section, we clarify how quite common notions are represented within this work. This is mainly to avoid confusion with seemingly common notations, that are introduced in the upcoming sections in a more rigorous way. Since all introduced notations and concepts are well known, we will only give an informal meaning.

Definition 2.1.1
A *function* from A to B, written $f : A \rightarrow B$, is a mapping, that assigns an element of B to each element of A. The set A is called *domain* and B is called *range*. □

Let us point out, that all functions used and defined in this work are total, i.e. they are defined on their whole domain.

The usual notations for set operations are used throughout the whole text. In particular we use the following:

Definition 2.1.2

- $\emptyset$ the empty set, i.e. a set without any elements,

- $\{a \in A \mid P(a)\}$ the set containing all elements of A, which satisfy property P,

- $\{f(b) \mid b \in B\}$ the set containing the image of a function f restricted to a set B,

- $A \cap B$ intersection of the sets A and B, and $\bigcap_{i \in I} A_i$ describing the (possibly infinite) intersection of some indexed sets,

- $A \cup B$ union of the sets A and B, and analogously $\bigcup_{i \in I} A_i$ describing the (possibly infinite) union of some indexed sets,

- $A \setminus B$ complement of B in A,

- $A \times B$ the Cartesian product of A and B. □

In order to keep notational overhead due to bookkeeping to a minimum, we use two special sets to denote natural numbers. Of which one contains the element 0 and the other does not.

Definition 2.1.3

The set of natural numbers is defined as $\mathbb{N}_0 := \{0, 1, 2, \ldots\}$ and the set of nonzero natural numbers as $\mathbb{N} := \{1, 2, 3, \ldots\}$. □

Let us already point out, that in most cases –like the upcoming definition of sequences– the positive natural numbers $\mathbb{N}$ is used as index set. This allows to encode initial states with the special index 0, removing extra treatments of those cases.

Definition 2.1.4 (tuples/sequences)

A *tuple* on a set V of length $n = \#\bar{v}$ is a function $\bar{v} : \{1, \dots n\} \to S$, they are represented in the usual tuple notation $\bar{v} = (v_1, \dots, v_n)$.

Likewise a *sequence* on a set S is a function $\mathbf{s} : \mathbb{N} \to S$. Sequences are represented in the usual way, either as compact notation $\mathbf{s} = (s_i)_{i \in \mathbb{N}}$ or as "infinite tuple" $\mathbf{s} = (s_1, s_2, \dots)$. □

Definition 2.1.5

- Two tuples $\bar{v}$, $\bar{w}$ are identical, iff they have the same length, i.e. $\#\bar{v} = \#\bar{w}$ and all their components are identical, i.e. $s_i = t_i$ for all $1 \leq i \leq \#\bar{v}$.

- Analogously two sequences $\mathbf{s}$ and $\mathbf{t}$ are equal, written $\mathbf{s} = \mathbf{t}$, iff their components agree, i.e. $s_i = t_i$ for all $i \in \mathbb{N}$.

- A sequence $\mathbf{s} = (s_i)_{i \in \mathbb{N}}$ has the *finite restriction*

$$\mathbf{s}|_n = (s_1, \dots, s_n)$$

to a tuple of length n. □

Definition 2.1.6

A partition $(P_1, \dots P_n)$ of a set S is tuple of disjoint subsets of S, dividing all members of the set in the members of the collection, i.e.

$$\bigcup_{i \in I} P_i = S \text{ and } P_i \cap P_j = \emptyset \text{ for all } i \in I \; (P_i \subseteq S \text{ already follows}).$$
□

Finally, to ease up several tedious inductive definitions, we make use of a tool used in theoretical computer science to formally specify context-free languages. Details of this notation can be found e.g. in [BBG+63] and [Sch08]

Definition 2.1.7 (Backus–Naur form)

For two sets T (terminals) and N (non-terminals), a grammar is a collection of rules that have the form

$$n ::= s_1 \ldots s_n,$$

where $n \in N$ and $s_i \in T \cup N$ for all $1 \leq i \leq n$.

The rule means, that the non-terminal n can be substituted by the string $s_1 \ldots s_n$, which might contain more non-terminals. The language L derived from a starting symbol $s \in N$ is the set of all strings of terminals, that can be derived from s by successively substituting all occurrences of nonterminals according to the given rules.

Notice, that there might be multiple rules for each non-terminal. Hence, to ease notation further, we adapt two common abbreviations that allow collecting rules for the same non-terminal into the same line:

Firstly we use the symbol " $|$ " to split several derivable strings and secondly we use " $a \underset{a \in A}{\Big|}$ " to add a derivation to each $a \in A \subseteq T$. $\square$

2.2 Semantics

One of the main tools we use is (generalised) semantics. In common use a semantics is applied to attach a meaning to a language. When dealing with controlled query evaluation however, it turns out, that in most cases the structure of the language is irrelevant. This is due to the fact, that most queries can be handled by only looking at the model class of the queried formula. Hence, we separate the structured parts, that mainly restrict the language with respect to its satisfaction symbol.

8

2.2.1 Generalized Semantics

As already stated, semantics in one of its most general forms is used:

Definition 2.2.1 (Semantics)

A semantics is a triple $(\mathcal{L}, \mathfrak{I}, \models)$, consisting of

- a *language* $\mathcal{L}$ (i.e. a non-empty set of strings on an alphabet),

- a class of *interpretations* $\mathfrak{I}$ (models) for that language and

- a *satisfaction relation* $\models \subseteq \mathfrak{I} \times \mathcal{L}$.

An element of the language is also called a *formula*. A formula $\varphi \in \mathcal{L}$ is satisfied in an interpretation $i \in \mathfrak{I}$, iff $(i, \varphi) \in \models$. As usual the standard notation $i \models \varphi$ is used, when a formula is satisfied, and $i \not\models \varphi$, when it is not. □

Throughout this work, only non-trivial semantics are discussed, i.e. the language, the class of interpretations and the satisfaction relation are non-empty (as sets).

There are two helpful addenda to the definition of satisfaction, to help in dealing with multiple formulae. The first is to allow sets of formulae on the right hand side, meaning that all of the contained formulae must be satisfied or unsatisfied simultaneously:

Definition 2.2.2

For $\mathcal{C} \subseteq \mathcal{L}$ and $i \in \mathfrak{I}$

- $i \models \mathcal{C}$ means that $i \models \varphi$ for all $\varphi \in \mathcal{C}$, and

- $i \overset{co}{\models} \mathcal{C}$ means that $i \not\models \varphi$ for all $\varphi \in \mathcal{C}$.

$\mathcal{C}$ is called *satisfiable*, iff there is an interpretation $i \in \mathfrak{I}$, s.t. $i \models \mathcal{C}$. □

The second tool is allowing sets of formulae on the left hand side, too, in order to deal simultaneously with all interpretations that satisfy or dissatisfy exactly all formulae contained in the specified sets.

To ease notation, the formulae that must be satisfied and those that must be dissatisfied can be handled as a bundle.

Definition 2.2.3 (Knowledge-Base)

A *Knowledge-base* on a semantics $\mathcal{S} = (\mathcal{L}, \mathfrak{I}, \vDash)$ is a pair $\mathcal{KK} = (\mathcal{T}_{\mathcal{KK}}, \mathcal{F}_{\mathcal{KK}})$, where

1. $\mathcal{T}_{\mathcal{KK}} \subseteq \mathcal{L}$ is the set of stored positive knowledge (or known true formulae).

2. $\mathcal{F}_{\mathcal{KK}} \subseteq \mathcal{L}$ is the set of stored negative knowledge (or known false formulae).

A knowledge-base is called *purely positive* [*purely negative*], iff no negative [positive] knowledge is stored, i.e. $\mathcal{F}_{\mathcal{KK}} = \emptyset$ [$\mathcal{T}_{\mathcal{KK}} = \emptyset$].

It is called *satisfiable* or *consistent*, iff there is an interpretation $i \in \mathfrak{I}$, s.t. $i \vDash \mathcal{T}_{\mathcal{KK}}$ and $i \overset{co}{\vDash} \mathcal{F}_{\mathcal{KK}}$. In this case, i is called interpretation of the knowledge-base, written $i \vDash \mathcal{KK}$. □

Definition 2.2.4 (Semantical Implication)

Given a fixed semantics $(\mathcal{L}, \mathfrak{I}, \vDash)$ and sets of formulae $\mathcal{T}, \mathcal{F}, \mathcal{R} \subseteq \mathcal{L}$, we define:

- $\mathcal{T}, \mathcal{F}$ *semantically imply* $\mathcal{R}$, written $\mathcal{T}, \mathcal{F} \vDash \mathcal{R}$, iff

$$\{i \in \mathfrak{I} \mid i \vDash \mathcal{T}\} \cap \{i \in \mathfrak{I} \mid i \overset{co}{\vDash} \mathcal{F}\} \subseteq \{i \in \mathfrak{I} \mid i \vDash \mathcal{R}\}$$

i.e. all interpretations which satisfy all formulae in $\mathcal{T}$, but none of $\mathcal{F}$, also satisfy all formulae in $\mathcal{F}$.

10

- $\mathcal{T}, \mathcal{F}$ *semantically co-imply* $\mathcal{R}$, written $\mathcal{T}, \mathcal{F} \overset{co}{\models} \mathcal{R}$, iff

$$\emptyset \neq \{i \in \mathfrak{I} \mid i \models \mathcal{T}\} \cap \{i \in \mathfrak{I} \mid i \overset{co}{\models} \mathcal{F}\} \subseteq \{i \in \mathfrak{I} \mid i \overset{co}{\models} \mathcal{R}\}$$

i.e. none of the interpretations, satisfying all formulae in $\mathcal{T}$, but none in $\mathcal{F}$, satisfies any formula of $\mathcal{R}$.

- for two knowledge-bases $(\mathcal{T}_0, \mathcal{F}_0), (\mathcal{T}_1, \mathcal{F}_1)$, *semantical implication* $\mathcal{T}_0, \mathcal{F}_0 \models \mathcal{T}_1, \mathcal{F}_1$ is given by

$$\{i \in \mathfrak{I} \mid i \models (\mathcal{T}_0, \mathcal{F}_0)\} \subseteq \{i \in \mathfrak{I} \mid i \models (\mathcal{T}_1, \mathcal{F}_1)\}\}$$

which is equivalent to

$$\{i \in \mathfrak{I} \mid i \models \mathcal{T}_0\} \cap \{i \in \mathfrak{I} \mid i \overset{co}{\models} \mathcal{F}_0\}$$
$$\subseteq \{i \in \mathfrak{I} \mid i \models \mathcal{T}_1\} \cap \{i \in \mathfrak{I} \mid i \overset{co}{\models} \mathcal{F}_1\} \quad \square$$

In the definition above the set $\mathcal{T}$ acts as set of positive knowledge, containing all facts known to be true. The contrasting set $\mathcal{F}$ acts as negative knowledge, containing all facts known to be false. For the sake of simplification, set brackets on the right side can be always omitted. The set brackets on the left are necessary to distinct between positive and negative knowledge. However, in case the set of negative knowledge $\mathcal{F}$ is empty, the set or its brackets may be omitted.

Lemma 2.2.5

For $\mathcal{T}, \mathcal{F} \subseteq \mathcal{L}$, the pair $(\mathcal{T}, \mathcal{F})$ is satisfiable, iff

$$\mathcal{T}, \mathcal{F} \overset{co}{\models} \emptyset \qquad \square$$

PROOF It holds $\{i \in \mathfrak{I} \mid i \stackrel{co}{\models} \emptyset\} = \mathfrak{I}$. Hence, any $i \in \mathfrak{I}$, s.t. $i \models \mathcal{T}$ and $i \stackrel{co}{\models} \mathcal{F}$ will witness $\emptyset \neq \{i \in \mathfrak{I} \mid i \models \mathcal{T}\} \cap \{i \in \mathfrak{I} \mid i \stackrel{co}{\models} \mathcal{F}\}$.

The other direction follows by reversing the argument. ∎

Remark 2.2.6

In the definition of semantical co-implication the set of interpretations of $\mathcal{T}$ violating (i.e. do not satisfy) all formulae in $\mathcal{F}$ may not be empty. This is mainly a technical trick, to achieve simpler definitions of the database-evaluators.

Also the notion of being a semantical co-implication is stronger than just not being a semantical implication: $\mathcal{T}, \mathcal{F} \not\models \mathcal{R}$ only means, that there is an interpretation $i \in \mathfrak{I}$, s.t. $i \models \mathcal{T}$ and $i \stackrel{co}{\models} \mathcal{F}$, but $i \not\models \mathcal{R}$. However, it allows interpretations to exist, where this does not hold, i.e. there still can be $j \in \mathfrak{I}$, s.t. $j \models \mathcal{T}$, $j \stackrel{co}{\models} \mathcal{F}$ and $j \models \mathcal{R}$. Semantic co-implication forbids this existence. Furthermore, it requires that especially $\mathcal{T}$ has at least one interpretation.

Hence, the symbols $\not\models$ and $\stackrel{co}{\models}$ should not be misinterpreted (likewise the symbols $\models$ and $\stackrel{co}{\not\models}$). □

Definition 2.2.7

The set of tautologies $\mathcal{T}_{\mathcal{S}}$ (always true formulae) and the set of unsatisfiables $\mathcal{F}_{\mathcal{S}}$ (always false formulae) are defined by

$$\mathcal{T}_{\mathcal{S}} := \{\varphi \in \mathcal{L} \mid \text{ for all } i \in \mathfrak{I} \; i \models \varphi\}$$

$$\mathcal{F}_{\mathcal{S}} := \{\varphi \in \mathcal{L} \mid \text{ for all } i \in \mathfrak{I} \; i \not\models \varphi\}$$ □

2.2.2 Structural properties

In some cases it does matter, if a language has special properties. Mainly it concerns the possession of operators on the language, that allow the language to internalise some of the properties of the satisfaction relation. In some settings, those operators allow a simplification of the censoring systems presented in chapter 5, namely if negation is internalised into the language. In other cases, e.g. if the language is atomic, they can cause problems if some additional knowledge is introduced to the setting as well.

Definition 2.2.8 (Subboolean language)
A language $\mathcal{L}$ is called *subboolean*, iff there are

- a non-empty, finite set of *operators* $\mathfrak{O}$ on $\mathcal{L}$,
  i.e. $o \in \mathfrak{O}$ is a function $o : \mathcal{L}^{\deg(o)} \to \mathcal{L}$ for some $\deg(o) \in \mathbb{N}$,

- and a *basis* $\mathfrak{B} \subseteq \mathcal{L}$, i.e. for all $o \in \mathfrak{O}$ and $\psi_1, \dots, \psi_{\deg(o)} \in \mathfrak{B}$

$$o(\psi_1, \dots, \psi_{\deg(o)}) \notin \mathfrak{B}$$

s.t. $\mathcal{L} = \bigcup_{i \in \mathbb{N}_0} \mathcal{L}_n$, where $\mathcal{L}_n$ is inductively defined by

- $\mathcal{L}_0 := \mathfrak{B}$ and

- $\mathcal{L}_{n+1} := \mathcal{L}_n \cup \bigcup_{o \in \mathfrak{O}} \{o(\psi_1, \dots, \psi_{\deg(o)}) \mid \psi_1, \dots, \psi_{\deg(o)} \in \mathcal{L}_n\}$.

The formulae contained in $\mathfrak{B}$ are called *base formulae* and the formulae in $\mathcal{L} \setminus \mathfrak{B}$ are called *compound formulae* of $\mathcal{L}$. □

Definition 2.2.9

A semantics $(\mathcal{L}, \mathfrak{I}, \vDash)$ is called *subboolean*, iff its language is sub-boolean and the satisfaction of compound formulae can be inductively calculated from the base formulae and Boolean functions assigned to the operators. I.e.

- for each operator $o \in \mathfrak{O}$ there is a Boolean function

$$b_o : \{0,1\}^{\deg(o)} \to \{0,1\},$$

- to each interpretation $i \in \mathfrak{I}$ and formula $\psi \in \mathcal{L}$ there are values $v_\psi^i \in \{0,1\}$, s.t. $v_\psi^i = 1$ iff $i \vDash \psi$ and $v_\psi^i = 0$ iff $i \nvDash \psi$,

- and the values v_ψ^i can be obtained by

    - if $\psi \in \mathfrak{B} = \mathcal{L}_0$,

        then $v_\psi^i = 1$ iff $i \vDash \psi$ and $v_\psi^i = 0$ iff $i \nvDash \psi$

    - if $\psi = o(\psi_1, \ldots, \psi_{\deg(o)}) \in \mathcal{L}_{n+1} \setminus \mathcal{L}_n$,

        then $v_\psi^i = b_o(v_{\psi_1}^i, \ldots, v_{\psi_{\deg(o)}}^i)$. $\qquad \square$

14

Definition 2.2.10 (Atomicity)

A subboolean semantics $(\mathcal{L}, \mathfrak{I}, \vDash)$ is called *atomic*, iff the sets of interpretations of sets of basic formulae are independent. I.e. for all $\mathcal{C}_1, \mathcal{C}_2 \subseteq \mathfrak{B}$ the conditions

- $\mathcal{C}_1, \mathcal{C}_2$ are semantic separable, i.e.

$$\{i \in \mathfrak{I} \mid i \vDash \mathcal{C}_1\} \neq \{i \in \mathfrak{I} \mid i \overset{co}{\vDash} \mathcal{C}_2\}$$

- and $\mathcal{C}_1, \mathcal{C}_2$ are semantic inclusive, i.e.

$$\mathcal{C}_1 \subseteq \mathcal{C}_2 \text{ iff } \mathcal{C}_2 \vDash \mathcal{C}_1$$

hold. □

Remark 2.2.11

One immediate property of atomicity is, that no basic formula $\psi \in \mathfrak{B}$ can be a tautology or unsatisfiable. Otherwise, either

$$\{i \in \mathfrak{I} \mid i \vDash \{\psi\}\} \neq \{i \in \mathfrak{I} \mid i \overset{co}{\vDash} \emptyset\}$$
$$\text{or } \{i \in \mathfrak{I} \mid i \vDash \emptyset\} \neq \{i \in \mathfrak{I} \mid i \overset{co}{\vDash} \{\psi\}\}$$

would be violated.

It is also worth noticing, that from the definition follows

$$\{i \in \mathfrak{I} \mid i \vDash \mathcal{C}_1\} = \{i \in \mathfrak{I} \mid i \vDash \mathcal{C}_2\} \text{ iff } \mathcal{C}_1 = \mathcal{C}_2$$

as well, for all $\mathcal{C}_1, \mathcal{C}_2 \subseteq \mathfrak{B}$. □

Example 2.2.12

As simple example consider the semantics $(\mathcal{L}, \mathfrak{I}, \vDash)$, with

- $\mathcal{L} := \{a, b\}^\star$
  $= \{\varepsilon, a, b, aa, ab, ba, bb, aaa, aab, aba, aab, abb, bbb, \ldots\}$

- $\mathfrak{I} := \{\mathfrak{k}, \mathfrak{j}\}$ and

- $\models := \{(\mathfrak{k}, a), (\mathfrak{j}, b)\} \cup \{(\mathfrak{k}, w), (\mathfrak{j}, w) \mid w \in \mathcal{L} \setminus \{a, b, \varepsilon\}\}$.

This semantics is subboolean with base formulae $\mathfrak{B} := \{\varepsilon, a, b\}$ and a single operator $\mathrm{concat}(\psi_1, \psi_2) = \psi_1 \psi_2$ and $b_{\mathrm{concat}} = \max(v_1, v_2)$. However, since

$$\{i \in \mathfrak{I} \mid i \models \{a\}\} = \{i \in \mathfrak{I} \mid i \overset{co}{\models} \{b\}\} = \{\mathfrak{k}\}$$

holds, it is not atomic (or alternatively, because $\varepsilon \in \mathfrak{B}$ is unsatisfiable and remark 2.2.11). □

Definition 2.2.13

A knowledge-base $\mathcal{KK} = (\mathcal{T}, \mathcal{F})$ on an atomic semantics is called *atomic*, iff $\mathcal{T}, \mathcal{F} \subseteq \mathfrak{B}$. □

A semantics defines truth and falsity for any formula based on the model it is interpreted on. On most common languages exists a special unary negation operator. The corresponding semantics internalize this operator by interchanging this truth and falsity of a formula within a model into the language.

Definition 2.2.14 (negation operator)

A semantics $(\mathcal{L}, \mathfrak{I}, \models)$ has a *negation operator* $\neg$, iff

- $\mathcal{L}$ is closed under $\neg$, i.e. $\varphi \in \mathcal{L}$ iff $\neg\varphi \in \mathcal{L}$.

- and for each $\varphi \in \mathcal{L}$ and $i \in \mathfrak{I}$, it holds $i \models \varphi$ iff $i \not\models \neg\varphi$. □

It is worth noticing, that $\neg$ might not be an explicit symbol of the language. In view of the given definition, it could also be a complex transformation of the formula, e.g. $\neg(\varphi) = \varphi \to \bot$ in sequential style propositional logics.

Remark 2.2.15

The converse of the second negation property, for each $\varphi \in \mathcal{L}$ and $i \in \mathfrak{I}$ it is

$$i \vDash \neg\varphi \text{ iff } i \nvDash \varphi,$$

also holds:

Otherwise either both, $i \vDash \neg\varphi$ and $i \vDash \varphi$, violating the resulting $i \nvDash \neg\varphi$, or both, $i \nvDash \neg\varphi$ and $i \nvDash \varphi$, violating $i \vDash \varphi$, would hold. □

Example 2.2.16 (2.2.12 cont'd)

There is a way to modify the presented into an atomic version. One can add a second operator to the set of operators, particularly a negation defined element-wise by

$$\neg\varepsilon = ab$$
$$\neg a = b$$
$$\neg b = a$$
$$\neg w = \varepsilon$$

for all $w \in \mathcal{L} \setminus \{\varepsilon, a, b\}$. Seeing that this is a negation is a straight forward check of satisfaction in the two interpretations:

$$\mathfrak{k} \vDash a \text{ and } \mathfrak{k} \nvDash \neg a$$
$$\mathfrak{k} \vDash w \text{ and } \mathfrak{k} \nvDash \neg w$$
$$\mathfrak{j} \vDash b \text{ and } \mathfrak{j} \nvDash \neg b$$
$$\mathfrak{j} \vDash w \text{ and } \mathfrak{j} \nvDash \neg w$$

Obviously, the Boolean function $b_\neg(v) := 1 - v$ can be assigned to the negation operator. Together with the operator concat a possible

17

choice of base formulae is $\mathfrak{B} := \{a\}$, which is trivially atomic. Notice, that $\varepsilon = \neg(\text{concat}(\neg(a), a))$ is not an element of the basis anymore, but can be expressed in terms of the basis and the operators as presented. □

2.3 Incomplete Evaluation

The second main tool is incomplete evaluation. The incomplete evaluator qualifies, to what extend a formula is known within a knowledge-base. An evaluated formula that is known, i.e. is either semantically implied or co-implied, can be evaluated to t (known to be true) or f (known to be false). But also a third option is possible, namely that the formula is not known. This is denoted by an evaluation u (unknown).

Definition 2.3.1 (Incomplete Evaluator)
Let $(\mathcal{L}, \mathfrak{I}, \vDash)$ be a semantics. The *full incomplete evaluator* $\text{eval}(\cdot)$ on this semantics is defined by:

$$
\text{eval} : \begin{cases} \wp(\mathcal{L}) \times \wp(\mathcal{L}) \times \mathcal{L} & \to & \{t, f, u\} \\[2mm] (\mathcal{T}, \mathcal{F}, \varphi) & \mapsto & \begin{cases} t & \text{if} & \mathcal{T}, \mathcal{F} \vDash \varphi \\ f & \text{if} & \mathcal{T}, \mathcal{F} \stackrel{co}{\vDash} \varphi \\ u & \text{else} \end{cases} \end{cases}
$$

The positive *incomplete evaluator* $\text{eval}(\cdot)$ on this semantics is defined by

$$\text{eval}: \begin{cases} \wp\left(\mathcal{L}\right) \times \mathcal{L} & \to & \{t, f, u\} \\[2mm] (\mathcal{T}, \varphi) & \mapsto & \begin{cases} t & \text{if} & \mathcal{T}, \emptyset \vDash \varphi \\ f & \text{if} & \mathcal{T}, \emptyset \overset{co}{\vDash} \varphi \\ u & \text{else} \end{cases} \end{cases}$$

with a different signature.

For any given knowledge-base $(\mathcal{T}, \mathcal{F})$. the short-notation $\text{eval}_{(\mathcal{T}, \mathcal{F})}$ is declared by

$$\text{eval}_{(\mathcal{T}, \mathcal{F})}(\varphi) = \text{eval}(\mathcal{T}, \mathcal{F}, \varphi)$$

and $\text{eval}_{\mathcal{T}}$ is declared by

$$\text{eval}_{\mathcal{T}}(\varphi) = \text{eval}(\mathcal{T}, \varphi) = \text{eval}(\mathcal{T}, \emptyset, \varphi) \qquad \square$$

Both definitions of eval are highly dependent on the underlying semantics. Thus, in case changing semantics are observed, one should add the currently used semantics into its signature. However, since in this work the actually used semantics is fixed in most situations, it is omitted in favour of readability.

Remark 2.3.2

As is easily seen, for any $\mathcal{C} \subseteq \mathcal{L}$ $\text{eval}_{\mathcal{C}}$ is a function: a formula $\varphi \in \mathcal{L}$ is evaluated to t, iff all interpretations $i \in \mathfrak{I}$ of $\mathcal{C}$ ($i \vDash \mathcal{C}$) are also interpretations of φ ($i \vDash \varphi$). It is evaluated to f, iff none of them is an interpretation of φ ($i \nvDash \varphi$).

Especially φ is evaluated to u, iff there are interpretations $i, \mathfrak{k} \in \mathfrak{I}$, s.t. $i \vDash \mathcal{C}$ and $\mathfrak{k} \vDash \mathcal{C}$, but $i \vDash \varphi$ and $\mathfrak{k} \nvDash \varphi$. $\qquad \square$

2.4 Censors for Databases

2.4.1 Databases

There are several different approaches to querying databases. A well-known possibility are databases for so-called retrieval queries, i.e. queries that formalize a predicate and databases returning a list of elements which satisfy this predicate.

Another approach is to consider Boolean queries, i.e. queries formalizing questions that can be answered with true (t) or false (f). Of course, since almost no knowledge-base is omniscient, there are questions that the database cannot decide by means of its stored (and supposedly true) information.

In this work we study the three-valued approach in a general framework and show how to apply it in the context of a database containing (incomplete) information. That means the decision whether a formula is evaluated to true, false or unknown is based on incomplete evaluation.

A general database, which is capable of answering true, false or unknown, can by formalized as follows:

Definition 2.4.1 (Boolean Database)
An (incomplete, generalized) Boolean database $D = (\mathcal{S}_D, \mathcal{T}_D, \mathcal{F}_D)$ is a semantics $\mathcal{S}_D$, together with a knowledge-base $(\mathcal{T}_D, \mathcal{F}_D)$ on $\mathcal{S}_D$.
A Boolean database is called *complete* iff u is not in the range of $\mathsf{eval}_{(\mathcal{T}_D, \mathcal{F}_D)}$.
A Boolean database E is a sub-database of D, iff $\mathcal{S}_D = \mathcal{S}_E$ and

$$\mathcal{T}_D, \mathcal{F}_D \vDash \mathcal{T}_E, \mathcal{F}_E.$$

□

General Boolean databases are only useful, if the underlying semantics is subject to change. Most times in this work, the semantics will be fixed throughout every chapter.

Remark 2.4.2

In semantics with a negation operator it is sufficient to store only the positive knowledge. This is simply done by adding negated versions of the false formulae to the set of positive knowledge. Also, it suffices to consider the positive evaluator only in this setting. In essence, in any logic with negation operator, all databases can be treated to be purely positive (or purely negative). □

There are mainly two ways to query a Boolean database: An agent can ask a formula of the database's semantics, then receive the result and maybe follow up to continue asking, or the agent can ask several queries at once and get a mapping of the query-set to the results.

However, since there is always an order in which the evaluation has to happen, the second way reduces to the first as well.

Definition 2.4.3 (Queries and Results)

- A *query* on a Boolean database D is a formula in the language of the database $q \in \mathcal{L}_D$. It has the *result* $r = \text{eval}_{(\mathcal{T}_D, \mathcal{F}_D)}(q)$.

- A *query-sequence* on a Boolean database D is a sequence

$$\mathbf{q} = (q_i)_{i \in \mathbb{N}} \in \mathcal{L}^{\mathbb{N}}.$$

It has the *result-sequence* $\mathbf{r} = (\text{eval}_{(\mathcal{T}_D, \mathcal{F}_D)}(q_i))_{i \in \mathbb{N}}$. □

Query sequences are particularly useful. They provide a handsome tool to simulate answering a stream of queries without the need to define an independent log. However, at a first glance they appear a bit counter-intuitive, since a guarding algorithm—having access to the modelled full stream of querryies—could "look into the future" and choose its answers dependent on this divination. To cope with this, we will introduce the quality-property of continuity (definition 2.4.19), that restricts an answer determination to past information.

2.4.2 Censors

When talking about privacy, we need to specify not only what is to be kept secret, but also which means can be used to achieve it. We make use of three knowledge-bases, namely

- the (incomplete) *knowledge-base* C_K (Censored Knowledge) concealed behind the censor,

- the *a priori-knowledge* A_K (Attacker's Knowledge) describing the (incomplete and restricted) knowledge of the attacker (which, in this work, is shared with the censor), and

- the (not necessarily satisfiable) *secrets* S_K (Secret Knowledge) containing protected formulae.

Here we mean by protected that after any sequence of queries none of the formulae contained in S_K may be revealed to the attacker. For the sake of simplicity we will assume that the attacker believes at the beginning only in true statements, i.e. we will assume $C_K \models A_K$.

Definition 2.4.4 (Privacy Configuration)

A *privacy configuration* on a semantics $\mathcal{S} = (\mathcal{L}, \mathfrak{I}, \vDash)$ is a triple

$$\mathcal{PC} = (\mathcal{CK}, \mathcal{AK}, \mathcal{SK}),$$

where $\mathcal{CK}$ (Censored Knowledge), $\mathcal{AK}$ (Attacker's Knowledge) and $\mathcal{SK} = (\mathcal{T}_{\mathcal{SK}}, \mathcal{F}_{\mathcal{SK}})$ (Secret Knowledge, divided in positive and negative secrets) are knowledge-bases on $\mathcal{S}$, s.t.

PC-A) $\mathcal{CK} \vDash \mathcal{AK}$ (Truthful Start).

PC-B) $\mathcal{CK}$ is satisfiable (Consistency).

PC-C) $\mathcal{AK} \nvDash \sigma$ for all $\sigma \in \mathcal{T}_{\mathcal{SK}}$ and $\mathcal{AK} \overset{co}{\nvDash} \sigma$ for all $\sigma \in \mathcal{F}_{\mathcal{SK}}$ (Hidden Secrets). □

Notably, the secret knowledge $\mathcal{SK}$ does not need to be satisfiable. Moreover, it can even be very unsatisfiable, i.e. it contains formulae that are not simultaneously satisfiable, or even have the same set of formulae as positive and negative secrets, i.e. $\mathcal{T}_{\mathcal{SK}} = \mathcal{F}_{\mathcal{SK}}$.

Remark 2.4.5

As a consequence of 2.4.4, the (supposed) pre-knowledge of the querying agent $\mathcal{AK}$ is satisfiable as well:
Either as a direct consequence of PC-C) by the definition of $\overset{co}{\vDash}$, or by combining the properties PC-A) and PC-B), since an interpretation of $\mathcal{CK}$ is also one for $\mathcal{AK}$. □

To achieve protection of the secret formulae, it is obviously necessary to disallow a querying agent to directly access the database, i.e. the database's evaluator. Moreover, one might want to add the possibility of returning an answer differing from the full truth, but might stay "close to" it. In particular, we want a mechanism that responds to a querying agent in such a way, that after any sequence of queries all secrets remain safely hidden. To this end, we add a new function, called *censor* to the database, that acts as mediator between a querying agent and the full stored information. As stated before, the censor also needs to see what the querying agent has as its a priori knowledge. Hence, it not only can make use of the query-sequence and access to the evaluation function of the database, but also sees the contextual information stored in the privacy-configuration.

Definition 2.4.6 (Censor)

A *censor* for a semantics $\mathcal{S}$ is a mapping that assigns an answering function

$$\mathsf{censor}_{\mathcal{PC}} : \mathcal{L}^{\mathbb{N}} \to \mathbb{A}^{\mathbb{N}}$$

to each given privacy configuration $\mathcal{PC} = (\mathcal{CK}, \mathcal{AK}, \mathcal{SK})$ on $\mathcal{S}$.
The set $\mathbb{A}$ contains the potential answers a censor might give.
Given a query-sequence $\mathbf{q} \in \mathcal{L}^{\mathbb{N}}$, the sequence

$$\mathbf{a} = \mathsf{censor}_{\mathcal{PC}}(\mathbf{q}) = (a_i)_{i \in \mathbb{N}} \in \mathbb{A}^{\mathbb{N}}$$

is called *answer-sequence* of censor given $\mathcal{PC}$. □

Typically, only $\{t, f, u, r\}$ and $\{t, f, u\}$ are choices for $\mathbb{A}$.
This coincides with the structure of the result-sequences. The first variant just adds a special symbol r (refusal) to the set of possible outcomes, to provide a syntactical representation of refusing to give any answer.

So far a censor can randomly answer and does not provide any safety.

24

Example 2.4.7 (Evaluation Censors)

A trivial censor is the revealing evaluation censor that assigns the actual answer to each query:

$$\mathsf{censor}_{(\mathcal{C\!K},\mathcal{A\!K},\mathcal{S\!K})}(\mathbf{q}) = (\mathsf{eval}(\mathcal{C\!K}, q_i))_{i \in \mathbb{N}}$$

A better, but also not very convenient censor is the overprotective evaluation censor given by

$$\mathsf{censor}_{(\mathcal{C\!K},\mathcal{A\!K},\mathcal{S\!K})}(\mathbf{q}) = (\mathsf{eval}(\mathcal{A\!K}, q_i))_{i \in \mathbb{N}}$$

that tells the attacker only answers that it could calculate itself. □

Clearly, neither the trivial nor the overprotective censor is of any use. However, to introduce quality properties of censors, we will have to define several additional helper structures.

2.4.3 Logging and Handling Facilities: Clouds

To effectively decide what answer should be chosen next by a censor, it is necessary to reflect not only the current view presented to a querying agent, but also keep track of the change of that views. Since an attacker is often enough quite aware that a database is censored, the information how the censor tries to change the attacker's believe, might be used to gain knowledge of an actually stored secret. Hence, in this section we introduce tools to model the believe of the querying agent after every stage of answering. To achieve this, we build up a meta-semantics called *cloud* and introduce a translation of truth meanings from given answers into the newly built up language.

Throughout this section, we fix a semantics $\mathcal{S} = (\mathcal{L}, \mathfrak{I}, \vDash)$.

Definition 2.4.8 (Cloud Formulae)

A *cloud-formula* is a formula of $\mathcal{L}$, prefixed by exactly one of the symbols $\Box$, $\blacksquare$, $\Diamond$ or $\blacklozenge$. Hence, the set of cloud-formulae over $\mathcal{L}$ is given by

$$\mathcal{CL} := \{\Box\psi, \blacksquare\psi, \Diamond\psi, \blacklozenge\psi \mid \psi \in \mathcal{L}\}$$

□

Definition 2.4.9 (Cloud)

A $(\mathcal{S}\text{-})$ *cloud* is a pair $\mathfrak{C} = (W_\mathfrak{C}, \iota_\mathfrak{C})$, where

- $W_\mathfrak{C}$ is a nonempty set of worlds (names of interpretations) and

- $\iota_\mathfrak{C} : W_\mathfrak{C} \to \mathfrak{I}$ is a function, i.e. for each $w \in W_\mathfrak{C}$, $\iota_\mathfrak{C}(w) \in \mathfrak{I}$ is an interpretation.

□

Introducing $\iota_\mathfrak{C}$ is actually unnecessary in this work, since it would suffice to store a set of interpretations directly. However, some proofs turn out to be more simple, when multiple names for the same interpretation can be used to keep track of different properties of that interpretation.

Clouds on a semantics, so far consisting of the shown prefixed formulae as cloud-language and a set of cloud-interpretations, essentially consisting of subsets of the preliminary interpretations, build— of course—another semantics. The satisfaction-relation for the cloud formulae is built up by modifying the underlying relation as follows:

Definition 2.4.10 ($\mathcal{CL}$-satisfiability)

Satisfiability of a formula $\Phi \in \mathcal{CL}$ within a $\mathcal{S}$-cloud $\mathfrak{C} = (W_\mathfrak{C}, \iota_\mathfrak{C})$ is given in the following way:

- $\mathfrak{C} \vDash \Box\psi$ iff for all $w \in W_\mathfrak{C}$ it is $\iota_\mathfrak{C}(w) \vDash \psi$

- $\mathfrak{C} \vDash \blacksquare\psi$ iff for all $w \in W_\mathfrak{C}$ it is $\iota_\mathfrak{C}(w) \nvDash \psi$

- $\mathfrak{C} \vDash \Diamond\psi$ iff there is a $w \in W_{\mathfrak{C}}$, s.t. $\iota_{\mathfrak{C}}(w) \vDash \psi$

- $\mathfrak{C} \vDash \blacklozenge\psi$ iff there is a $w \in W_{\mathfrak{C}}$, s.t. $\iota_{\mathfrak{C}}(w) \nvDash \psi$

A formula Φ is valid iff it is satisfied in all $\mathcal{S}$-clouds. □

All notions of semantic implication defined in section 2.2 are extended to the thus newly built semantics. Especially, we make use of (cloud-) satisfaction of sets of cloud-formulae and semantic implication and co-implication of sets of formulae.

To provide a translation of a query's answer value to the new logging structure, we introduce a function, that assigns to each such pair an intended content.

Definition 2.4.11 (Content)
Let $\psi \in \mathcal{L}$ and $a \in \{t, f, u, r\}$. The (intended) *content* of a as answer to ψ is given by

$$
\text{Cont}(\psi, a) = \begin{cases}
\{\Box\psi\} & \text{if} \quad a = t \\
\{\blacksquare\psi\} & \text{if} \quad a = f \\
\{\Diamond\psi, \blacklozenge\psi\} & \text{if} \quad a = u \\
\emptyset & \text{if} \quad a = r
\end{cases}
$$

□

Remark 2.4.12
In case $\mathcal{L}$ is viewed in context of a semantics with a negation operator, the definition can be simplified to

$$
\text{Cont}(\psi, a) = \begin{cases}
\{\Box\psi\} & \text{if} \quad a = t \\
\{\Box\neg\psi\} & \text{if} \quad a = f \\
\{\Diamond\psi, \Diamond\neg\psi\} & \text{if} \quad a = u \\
\emptyset & \text{if} \quad a = r
\end{cases}
$$

27

So in fact, negative knowledge, denying a formula, is being transformed to positive knowledge, enforcing a negated formula. □

As already stated, meta inferences make dealing with contents more difficult. In chapter 5 we present situations, where a given answer changes the view of a querying agent in a harmful way. Specifically, it becomes able to infer actually stored values of queries, despite the fact, that a different value was given as answer. Hence, in order to keep track of the intended believe at each stage of answering (and hence also its change), we introduce a censor's state cloud, that strongly depends on the context where it is build up.

Definition 2.4.13 (StateCloud)
On a fixed Boolean database D, let censor be a censor and $\mathcal{PC} = (\mathcal{CK}, \mathcal{AK}, \mathcal{SK})$ be a privacy configuration. We define the *state cloud* wrt. a query-sequence $\mathbf{q} \in \mathcal{L}^{\mathbb{N}}$ at stage n by

$$\mathscr{HC}_{\mathcal{PC},\mathbf{q}}(n) := \bigcup_{\varphi \in \mathcal{AK}} \mathrm{Cont}(\varphi, t) \cup \bigcup_{i=1}^{n} \mathrm{Cont}(q_i, a_i),$$

where $\mathbf{a} := \mathsf{censor}_{(\mathcal{CK}, \mathcal{AK}, \mathcal{SK})}(\mathbf{q})$. □

Notice, that state clouds depend heavily on all available context information, i.e. privacy configuration, query sequence and the calculated answer-sequence.

2.4.4 Privacy: The Qualities of a Censor

There are two levels at which the quality of a censor can be measured. The first level involves the answers directly returned by the censor.

Since they provide a believe to any querying agent, they should be—
to some extend—believable, that is consistent. Also the provided
believe should not give away any secret. Otherwise, the censor would
appear useless.

On a second level, a censor should also fulfil more indirect concerns. To start with, it should stay as close to "the truth" as possible.
This means, it should provide as much actually stored information to
a querying agent as possible. Another concern is what happens if the
used algorithm is known to the attacker. This would induce, that the
attacker might be able to reverse engineer the decision process the
censor went through, possibly revealing a conditional necessity that
leaks a secret. Lastly, since the query-sequences we use are only
meant as a technical tool, answers should not depend on queries,
that will happen in the future.

Immediate Qualities

To formalize the first level of qualities, that the directly provided
believe system should have, in this section we introduce two quality
terms: *Credibility* and *Effectiveness*.

Credibility means, that the provided information is consistent at
any given point.

Definition 2.4.14 (Credible)

A censor censor is called *credible* for $\mathcal{PC}$, iff for every sequence $\mathbf{q} \in \mathcal{L}^{\mathbb{N}}$
and every $n \in \mathbb{N}$, it holds

$$\mathcal{HB}_{\mathcal{PC},\mathbf{q}}(n) \text{ is satisfiable} \qquad \left(C^n_{\mathcal{PC},\mathbf{q}} \right)$$

It is called *credible*, iff it is credible for all privacy-configurations.□

It is immediately clear, that a censor should not directly or almost directly give away the secrets. I.e. *effectiveness* is given, if any provided view does not imply the knowledge of any secret.

Definition 2.4.15 (Effective)

A censor censor is called *effective* for $\mathcal{PC} = (\mathcal{CK}, \mathcal{AK}, (\mathcal{T}_{\mathcal{SK}}, \mathcal{F}_{\mathcal{SK}}))$, iff for all sequences $\mathbf{q} \in \mathcal{L}^{\mathbb{N}}$ and every $n \in \mathbb{N}$ it holds

$$\mathscr{H}_{\mathcal{PC},\mathbf{q}}(n) \not\models \Box\sigma \text{ for every } \sigma \in \mathcal{T}_{\mathcal{SK}} \qquad \left(E_{\mathcal{PC},\mathbf{q}}^{n}\right)$$

and

$$\mathscr{H}_{\mathcal{PC},\mathbf{q}}(n) \not\models \blacksquare\sigma \text{ for every } \sigma \in \mathcal{F}_{\mathcal{SK}} \qquad \left(\bar{E}_{\mathcal{PC},\mathbf{q}}^{n}\right)$$

(i.e. no secret is semantically implied by a state cloud).

It is called *effective*, iff it is effective for all privacy-configurations.□

For technical reasons, mainly to allow inductive proofs, we also introduce a notion of *stages*. That is, the required properties of effectiveness and credibility are held for all answers up to a given point in the query-sequence.

Definition 2.4.16 (Stages)

A censor censor is called credible [effective] for $\mathcal{PC}$ up to stage $k \in \mathbb{N}$, iff the condition $\left(C_{\mathcal{PC},\mathbf{q}}^{n}\right)$ $[\left(E_{\mathcal{PC},\mathbf{q}}^{n}\right)$ and $\left(\bar{E}_{\mathcal{PC},\mathbf{q}}^{n}\right)]$, is satisfied for all $n \leq k$.

A censor is called credible [effective] up to stage $k \in \mathbb{N}$, if it is for all privacy-configurations. □

Example 2.4.17

The revealing evaluation censor from example 2.4.7 is credible, but not effective. The overprotective evaluation censor is effective and credible. The censor given by

$$\text{censor}_{\mathcal{PC}(\mathcal{O}_{\!C},\mathcal{A}_{\!C},\mathcal{S}_{\!C})}(\mathbf{q}) = \begin{cases} (f)_{i\in\mathbb{N}} & \text{if} \quad \mathcal{S}_{\!C} = (\emptyset,\emptyset) \\ (\text{eval}_{\mathcal{A}_{\!C}}(q_i))_{i\in\mathbb{N}} & \text{else} \end{cases}$$

is effective, but not credible. Effectiveness follows in the "else"-case by the definition of $\mathcal{PC}$, which implies $\text{eval}_{\mathcal{A}_{\!C}}(\sigma) \in \{f, u\}$ for all secrets $\sigma \in \mathcal{T}_{\mathcal{S}_{\!C}}$ and $\text{eval}_{\mathcal{A}_{\!C}}(\sigma) \in \{t, u\}$ for all secrets $\sigma \in \mathcal{F}_{\mathcal{S}_{\!C}}$. If there are no secrets this fact is trivial.

However the censor is not credible, since it will answer f to a query on a tautology or formula from $\mathcal{T}_{\mathcal{A}_{\!C}}$ in any privacy configuration with an empty set of secrets. □

Effective but not credible censors are, however, not very common. The presented censor for example is credible for all privacy configurations that protect at least one secret. Furthermore in the above construction one can mainly change the answering function in case no secrets are to be protected and change to a different effective and credible censor in case there is something to be kept secret. This is due to the fact that, if the censors' answers lead to an unsatisfiable state cloud at stage n, for any positive [negative] secret σ (in fact for any formula $\sigma \in \mathcal{L}$) it would follow $\mathcal{H}_{\mathcal{PC},\mathbf{q}}(n) \models \Box\sigma$ $[\mathcal{H}_{\mathcal{PC},\mathbf{q}}(n) \models \blacksquare\sigma]$ immediately, violating the property of effectiveness. To summarize this:

Lemma 2.4.18
Let $\mathcal{PC}$ be a privacy configuration, s.t. $\mathcal{S}_{\!C} \neq (\emptyset, \emptyset)$. Then every censor that is effective for $\mathcal{PC}$ is also credible for $\mathcal{PC}$. □

Meta Qualities

There are some properties one might deem useful or desirable for a censor. Those consist of properties, that restrict the censor in the choice of answers or add safety on a not immediate level. In this section, we introduce for the first category the notions *continuity*, *truthful* and its negation *lying* together with the variant *cooperation*, and *minimal invasion*. For the second kind, we introduce the term of *repudiation* and its more restricted atomic version.

Continuity is more a technical necessity, then a privacy condition. The definition of continuity is the usual term, that is also used in the standard sequence topology, where sets of sequences with identical initial sequences act as basis of the open sets.

Definition 2.4.19 (Continuous)

A censor censor is called *continuous* for a privacy-configuration $\mathcal{PC}$, iff for all sequences $\mathbf{q}, \mathbf{r} \in \mathcal{L}^{\mathbb{N}}$ and all $n \in \mathbb{N}$, it is

$$\mathbf{q}|_n = \mathbf{r}|_n \to \mathsf{censor}(\mathbf{q})|_n = \mathsf{censor}(\mathbf{r})|_n \quad ,$$

where $\mathbf{a}|_n$ denotes the initial segment of $\mathbf{a}$ of length n, i.e. $(a_1, \ldots, a_n)$. The censor is called *continuous*, iff it is continuous for all privacy-configurations. □

A censor being *truthful* translates to the requirement, that the censor should not make any querying agent believe something false.

Definition 2.4.20 (Truthful)

The censor censor is called *truthful*, iff for all privacy configurations $\mathcal{PC}$, for all question sequences $\mathbf{q}$ and for all i:

$$a_i \in \{r, \mathsf{eval}_{\mathcal{OC}}(q_i)\} \ ,$$

where $\mathbf{a} := \mathsf{censor}_{\mathcal{PC}}(\mathbf{q})$.
A censor that is not truthful is called *lying*. □

Minimal invasion means that the censor should only hide answers, that are directly harmful, i.e. answers leading to an inconsistent view or a view that implies a secret.

Definition 2.4.21 (Minimal Invasion)

Let the censor censor$_{\mathcal{PC}}$ be effective and credible for $\mathcal{PC}$.

It is called *minimally invasive* for $\mathcal{PC}$, iff whenever $a_i \neq \text{eval}_{\mathcal{OC}}(q_i)$ replacing a_i by $\text{eval}_{\mathcal{OC}}(q_i)$ would lead to a violation of either effectiveness or credibility. A censor is called *minimally invasive*, iff it is minimally invasive for all privacy-configurations. □

It might seem useful, that a censor should always honour a request for information, i.e. return an answer that is actually a possible evaluation. Although, this translates to either giving up on hiding information, and hence the intent of censoring, or to lie and not refuse whenever necessary. Obviously, in this work we make use of the second option.

Definition 2.4.22 (Cooperation)

A censor censor$_{\mathcal{PC}}$ is called *cooperative* in a privacy configuration $\mathcal{PC} = (\mathcal{OC}, \mathcal{AC}, \mathcal{SC})$, iff for all query-sequences $\mathbf{q}$ and indices $i \in \mathbb{N}$

$$r \neq \text{censor}_{\mathcal{PC}}(\mathbf{q})_i$$

I.e. r is not a possible answer for censor$_{\mathcal{PC}}$ □

In view of the fact that no algorithm can be hidden forever, an additional goal is to ensure that a continuous censor should provide unrevealing answers even if the method of determination is revealed and the attacker even knows the potential secrets. The condition of repudiation intuitively reads that there is a knowledge-base in which all secrets are (simultaneously) not stored (directly or indirectly) and, supplied to a censor, would produce the same answers as the original. Notice that this definition provides a version of plausible deniability to all secrets, depending on the query sequence.

Definition 2.4.23 (Repudiation)

A censor censor$_{\mathcal{RC}}$ is called *repudiating*, iff for each privacy configuration $(\mathcal{CK}, \mathcal{AK}, \mathcal{SK})$ and each query sequence $\mathbf{q}$ there are alternative knowledge-bases $\mathcal{RK}_i$, s.t.

R-A) for all $n \in \mathbb{N}$

$$\mathsf{censor}_{(\mathcal{CK}, \mathcal{AK}, \mathcal{SK})}(\mathbf{q})|_n = \mathsf{censor}_{(\mathcal{RK}_n, \mathcal{AK}, \mathcal{SK})}(\mathbf{q})|_n,$$

R-B) for all $n \in \mathbb{N}$ and all $\sigma \in \mathcal{T}_{\mathcal{SK}} : \mathcal{RK}_n \not\vdash \sigma$, and
for all $n \in \mathbb{N}$ and all $\sigma \in \mathcal{F}_{\mathcal{SK}} : \mathcal{RK}_n \not\vdash^{co} \sigma$,

R-C) for all $n \in \mathbb{N}$ $(\mathcal{RK}_n, \mathcal{AK}, \mathcal{SK})$ is a privacy configuration.

If in addition censor is defined on an atomic semantics, it is called *atomic repudiating*, iff. the knowledge-bases $\mathcal{RK}_n$ are atomic, too. □

Remark 2.4.24

The presented definition of (non atomic) repudiation works very well to protect the data in the general semantics. However, in case an attacker knows enough of the structure of the protected $\mathcal{CK}$ –e.g. if $\mathcal{CK}$ is atomic–, it turns out to be insufficient. □

Chapter 3

Example Semantics

3.1 Propositional Logic

Propositional logic is the most basic case for treating information. In various settings that deal with propositional data the following formalization is used: mostly all data that somehow can be called basic are modeled as propositional atoms. Then, making use of this basic structure, more complex formulae are evaluated.

Usually a (incomplete) propositional knowledge-base consists of these atoms and stores the information whether they are true or false, implicitly storing the rest as unknown. A knowledge-base of this kind, i.e. one that stores only atomic propositions and their truth values, is immediately *atomic* in the meaning given by definition 2.2.13. The evaluation of a complex formula depends on whether all assignments of the unknown atoms to true and false result in the same truth value for the complex formula. Consider, for instance, the formula $p \wedge q$. If p is unknown and q is false, then $p \wedge q$ will be evaluated to false since in both cases—p is true and p is false—the formula $p \wedge q$ will have the truth value false. However, if p is unknown and q is true, then the formula $p \wedge q$ will be evaluated to unknown since there is an assignment of p that makes $p \wedge q$ true and there is another assignment of p that makes $p \wedge q$ false.

In this work and especially with the censors in chapter 5, mostly general knowledge-bases are discussed, namely such that can store more complex formulae.

A careful examination of the literature on data privacy for propositional databases [BB04a, BB04b, BB07, BW08, BKS95, SDJR83] reveals that almost always only atomic databases are considered to settle the data privacy question.

This leads to several interesting questions.

1. Is the generalization from storing atomic to storing complex facts really necessary?

2. To what extent can the storage of facts be reduced / simplified?

3. Is it necessary for an attacking agent to know the atoms that are actually used in the knowledge-base?

In chapter 4 we will address the first two questions in an even more general context: With respect to the first question, it turns out that for each propositional knowledge-base, there exists a pseudo-atomic database and a translation such that the answer evaluation of a given query over the knowledge-base equals the evaluation of the translated query over the pseudo-atomic knowledge-base. This is established by showing that all query evaluations over a general database can be done via an evaluation function that only knows the truth values of certain base formulae. Hence these base formulae can then be translated to atomic formulae, which can be stored in an atomic database.

Furthermore, we establish that these sets of base formulae are minimal, which answers the first two questions partially: For propositional knowledge-bases it is always possible to store either the positive or the negative part as only atoms.

It also shows how switching to the atomic knowledge-bases simplifies query evaluation.

Since pseudo-atomic knowledge-bases act almost like fully atomic knowledge-bases, the third question can be answered: An attacking agent needs to at least know the atoms that are needed to encode the secrets, and it is irrelevant whether the knowledge-base internally uses a finer granularity.

3.1.1 Semantics

Since propositional logic is well known and discussed in literature, we give only a brief overview to help adapting to the used notations.

The semantics of propositional logic is given by

$$\mathbb{P}_\mathtt{A} = (\mathcal{L}_\mathtt{A}, \mathfrak{I}_\mathtt{A}, \vDash)$$

as presented below.

37

Language/Syntax

Definition 3.1.1

The language of propositional logic $\mathcal{L}_A$ over a set of propositional letters A is defined by the following Backus–Naur form:

$$\psi ::= a \underset{a \in A}{\big|} \quad | \quad (\neg \psi) \quad | \quad (\psi \wedge \psi)$$

The *length* $\#\psi$ of a propositional formula is defined to be the number of logical connectors $(\neg, \wedge)$ in the formula. □

To ease notation, brackets will be left away, whenever it is clear where they should be, e.g. outermost brackets.

Standard Interpretations

Constructing the set of interpretations happens to some extend in a reverse way of the definition of semantical implication in section 2.2. First it is declared, how a (complete) atomic knowledge-base semantically implies specific formulae. Afterwards this is generalized to gain a definition of the satisfaction relation. Then it normally proceeds by entailing all other defined uses, like e.g. general knowledge-bases.

Definition 3.1.2

The set of interpretations for $\mathbb{P}_A$ is the set of Boolean functions

$$\mathfrak{I}_A := \{ f \mid f : A \to \{0, 1\} \}.$$ □

Definition 3.1.3 (Atomic Semantic Implication)

Let $(\mathcal{T}_\mathbb{A}, \mathcal{F}_\mathbb{A})$ be a **partition** of $\mathbb{A}$. We will refer to the sets as true $(\mathcal{T}_\mathbb{A})$ and false $(\mathcal{F}_\mathbb{A})$ atoms, respectively.

Atomic semantic implication of a propositional formula $\psi \in \mathbb{P}_\mathbb{A}$ by $(\mathcal{T}_\mathbb{A}, \mathcal{F}_\mathbb{A})$, in symbols

$$\mathcal{T}_\mathbb{A}, \mathcal{F}_\mathbb{A} \vDash \psi,$$

is inductively defined as follows:

- $\mathcal{T}_\mathbb{A}, \mathcal{F}_\mathbb{A} \vDash a$ if $a \in \mathcal{T}_\mathbb{A}$

- $\mathcal{T}_\mathbb{A}, \mathcal{F}_\mathbb{A} \nvDash a$ if $a \in \mathcal{F}_\mathbb{A}$

- $\mathcal{T}_\mathbb{A}, \mathcal{F}_\mathbb{A} \vDash \neg\psi$ if $(\mathcal{T}_\mathbb{A}, \mathcal{F}_\mathbb{A}) \nvDash \psi$

- $\mathcal{T}_\mathbb{A}, \mathcal{F}_\mathbb{A} \nvDash \neg\psi$ if $(\mathcal{T}_\mathbb{A}, \mathcal{F}_\mathbb{A}) \vDash \psi$

- $\mathcal{T}_\mathbb{A}, \mathcal{F}_\mathbb{A} \vDash \psi_1 \wedge \psi_2$ if $(\mathcal{T}_\mathbb{A}, \mathcal{F}_\mathbb{A}) \vDash \psi_1$ and $(\mathcal{T}_\mathbb{A}, \mathcal{F}_\mathbb{A}) \vDash \psi_2$

- $\mathcal{T}_\mathbb{A}, \mathcal{F}_\mathbb{A} \nvDash \psi_1 \wedge \psi_2$ if $(\mathcal{T}_\mathbb{A}, \mathcal{F}_\mathbb{A}) \nvDash \psi_1$ or $(\mathcal{T}_\mathbb{A}, \mathcal{F}_\mathbb{A}) \nvDash \psi_2$ □

Definition 3.1.4 (Propositional Satisfiability)

For any Boolean function $\mathfrak{f} : \mathbb{A} \to \{0, 1\}$ let

- $\mathcal{T}_\mathbb{A}(\mathfrak{f}) := \{a \in \mathbb{A} \mid \mathfrak{f}(a) = 1\}$ and

- $\mathcal{F}_\mathbb{A}(\mathfrak{f}) := \{a \in \mathbb{A} \mid \mathfrak{f}(a) = 0\}$.

Then define

$$\mathfrak{f} \vDash \varphi, \text{ iff } \mathcal{T}_\mathbb{A}(\mathfrak{f}), \mathcal{F}_\mathbb{A}(\mathfrak{f}) \vDash \varphi.$$
□

Lemma 3.1.5 ($\models$ is well defined)

For all formulae $\varphi \in \mathbb{P}_A$ and all interpretations i

$$either\ i \models \varphi\ or\ i \not\models \varphi. \qquad \qquad \square$$

PROOF Straightforward by induction on the length of the formula.■

Definition 3.1.6

We extend the notion of satisfiability in the way given by the definitions 2.2.2 and 2.2.4 to semantic implication of sets of formulae and knowledge-bases. $\qquad \square$

Remark 3.1.7

Obviously, if semantical implication is restricted to sets of atomic propositional formulae on the left side and a single formula on the right side, then the semantical implication matches the definition of atomic semantic implication. $\qquad \square$

3.1.2 Basic Properties

Remark 3.1.8

Since $(\mathcal{T}_A, \mathcal{F}_A)$ is a partition of A, we obviously have

$$(\mathcal{T}_A, \mathcal{F}_A) \not\models \psi \text{ if and only if not } (\mathcal{T}_A, \mathcal{F}_A) \models \psi$$

for all formulae ψ. We will use the following easy-to-check properties without explicitly mentioning them:

- $(\mathcal{T}_A, \mathcal{F}_A) \models \psi$ iff $(\mathcal{T}_A, \mathcal{F}_A) \not\models \neg\psi$,

- $(\mathcal{T}_A, \mathcal{F}_A) \not\models \psi$ iff $(\mathcal{T}_A, \mathcal{F}_A) \models \neg\psi$,

- $\neg\psi \in \mathcal{T}_S$ iff $\psi \in \mathcal{F}_S$,

- $\psi \in \mathcal{T}_S$ iff $\neg\psi \in \mathcal{F}_S$,

- $\psi_1 \wedge \psi_2 \in \mathcal{T}_S$ iff $\psi_1, \psi_2 \in \mathcal{T}_S$ and

- $\psi_1 \wedge \psi_2 \in \mathcal{F}_S$ iff $\psi_i \in \mathcal{F}_S$ for at least one $i \in \{1, 2\}$ □

The next lemma is an immediate consequence of the presented definitions.

Lemma 3.1.9

Propositional logic is a subboolean, atomic semantics with negation. The base formulae $\mathfrak{B} = \mathtt{A}$ and operators $\mathfrak{O} = \{\neg, \wedge\}$, where $\neg$ is a negation operator. □

PROOF By construction, it is easy to see, that

- $b_\wedge(v_1, v_2) = \min(v_1, v_2)$ and

- $b_\neg(v) = 1 - v$

fulfil all requirements. ∎

3.2 Boolean Description Logic

Often, not only information has to be protected, that can be pressed into an atomic semantics, but also has structural information. One commonly used framework to model structural information is description logic. Since it has also the property of not being atomic in most of its varieties, it also provides a perfect basis to act as a running example to show how the censors discussed in chapter 5 answer. Hence, the goal of this section is to remind of the definition of Boolean $\mathcal{ALC}$ and build up a standard situation that can be used as common example.

41

It is also possible to define privacy in the original $\mathcal{ALC}$ as an ontological setup. Methods following this approach have been studied for example in [SS09] and [SS07].

3.2.1 Semantics

Language/Syntax

Despite the fact that $\mathcal{ALC}$ usually denotes only satisfiability of conceptual knowledge [BCM+03], namely T-Boxes, i.e. sets of subsumption statements, and A-Boxes, i.e. (positive) assertional statements about individuals, in this work Boolean $\mathcal{ALC}$ will mostly be referred to as $\mathcal{ALC}$ to adapt it to the used semantical view.

Definition 3.2.1 ($\mathcal{ALC}$)
Given two disjoint sets of symbols $\mathscr{AC}$ (atomic concepts) and $\mathscr{AR}$ (atomic roles), the language of $\mathcal{ALC}$ is defined by the following grammar in Backus–Naur form:

$$\psi ::= \psi \wedge \psi \mid \neg\psi \mid C \sqsubseteq C$$
$$C ::= C_i \underset{C_i \in \mathscr{AC}}{\mid} \quad \mid \perp \mid \top \mid C \sqcap C \mid \overline{C} \mid \exists R.C \mid \forall R.C$$
$$R ::= R_i \underset{R_i \in \mathscr{AR}}{\mid}$$

Here $C_i \in \mathscr{AC}$ are the atomic concepts and $R_i \in \mathscr{AR}$ are atomic roles (or role names). The sets $\mathcal{R}$ (Roles), $\mathcal{C}$ (Concepts) and $\mathcal{L}_{\mathcal{ALC}}$ ($\mathcal{ALC}$-formulae) are defined as the sets of words that can be derived starting from R, C and ψ respectively. Further we refer to a set of $\mathcal{ALC}$-formulae as (positive $\mathcal{ALC}$-) *knowledge-base* and to the pair $(\mathscr{AR}, \mathscr{AC})$ as its (*description*) *basis*. □

Interpretations

Definition 3.2.2 ($\mathcal{ALC}$-Interpretation)

Given a description basis $(\mathscr{AR}, \mathscr{AC})$, an ($\mathcal{ALC}$-) *interpretation* is a pair $(\Delta_{\mathcal{I}}, \cdot^{\mathcal{I}})$, consisting of a non-empty *domain* $\Delta_{\mathcal{I}}$ and a function

$$\cdot^{\mathcal{I}} : \mathcal{C} \cup \mathcal{R} \to \wp(\Delta_{\mathcal{I}}) \cup \wp(\Delta_{\mathcal{I}} \times \Delta_{\mathcal{I}})$$

that satisfies the following conditions:

- $\top^{\mathcal{I}} = \Delta_{\mathcal{I}}$, $\bot^{\mathcal{I}} = \emptyset$

- for each atomic concept $A \in \mathscr{AC}$: $A^{\mathcal{I}} \subseteq \Delta_{\mathcal{I}}$

- for each atomic role $R \in \mathscr{AR}$: $R^{\mathcal{I}} \subseteq \Delta_{\mathcal{I}} \times \Delta_{\mathcal{I}}$

- for each compound concept it inductively holds

  - $(C \sqcap D)^{\mathcal{I}} = C^{\mathcal{I}} \cap D^{\mathcal{I}}$
  - $(\overline{C})^{\mathcal{I}} = \Delta_{\mathcal{I}} \setminus C^{\mathcal{I}}$
  - $(\exists R.C)^{\mathcal{I}} = \{a \in \Delta_{\mathcal{I}} \mid \exists b \in C^{\mathcal{I}} : (a, b) \in R^{\mathcal{I}}\}$
  - $(\forall R.C)^{\mathcal{I}} = \{a \in \Delta_{\mathcal{I}} \mid \forall b \in \Delta_{\mathcal{I}} : (a, b) \in R^{\mathcal{I}} \to b \in C^{\mathcal{I}}\}$ □

Definition 3.2.3 ($\mathcal{ALC}$-Satisfiability)

Satisfiability of formulae within an interpretation $\mathcal{I} = (\Delta_{\mathcal{I}}, \cdot^{\mathcal{I}})$ is defined inductively as follows:

- $\mathcal{I} \models C \sqsubseteq D$ iff $C^{\mathcal{I}} \subseteq D^{\mathcal{I}}$

- $\mathcal{I} \models \neg\psi$ iff not $\mathcal{I} \models \psi$ (abbreviated by $\mathcal{I} \not\models \psi$)

- $\mathcal{I} \models \varphi \wedge \psi$ iff $\mathcal{I} \models \varphi$ and $\mathcal{I} \models \psi$ □

Remark 3.2.4

It should be clear now that expressions of the form $C \sqsubseteq D$ and $\overline{C} \sqcap D$ are of two different types. The expression $C \sqsubseteq D$ is a formula, which thus can be true of false; whereas $\overline{C} \sqcap D$ is a concept, which is interpreted as a set of objects. □

3.2.2 A Running Example

All censors of chapter 5 can be used to handle knowledge-bases on $\mathcal{ALC}$. In this section we present a standard situation to provide examples of how the censors would behave in it. The presented examples are a mainly a notational variant of the examples presented in [SW14].

To avoid over-complicating the example, we introduce straight forward and intuitive variants and short notations: For two concepts C and D and $(\mathcal{ALC}\text{-})$ formulae $\psi_1, \psi_2 \in \mathcal{L}_{\mathcal{ALC}}$

- $C \sqcup D$ abbreviates $\overline{(\overline{C} \sqcap \overline{D})}$,

- $C \sqsupseteq D$ abbreviates $D \sqsubseteq C$,

- $C \equiv D$ abbreviates $C \sqsubseteq D \wedge D \sqsubseteq C$,

- $\psi_1 \to \psi_2$ abbreviates $\neg(\psi_1 \wedge \neg\psi_2)$, and

- $\psi_1 \vee \psi_2$ abbreviates $\neg(\neg\psi_1 \wedge \neg\psi_2)$.

The semantical meaning of the abbreviations follows exactly the usual usage of these symbols (equivalence or union of sets, resp. logical implication or conjunction). Let us point out, that the first abbreviation is on the level of concepts and all others are short notations of formulae.

To start with the example setup, consider the following setting:
A community of six persons (all with drivers licence) shares two cars,
an Opol and a Persche. One day it happens that one of the cars was
photographed in a speeding-trap. The photograph clearly shows the
driver's hair colour and the car driven.

In order to determine who drove the car through the speed-trap the
policeman calls at the community to inquire. The gardener (a very
loyal employee) answers the phone.

In our terms we have the following situation: Both, $\mathcal{GK}$ (the knowledge of the gardener) and $\mathcal{AK}$ (the knowledge of the inquiring policeman), contain the following information:

- Alice, Bob, Carol, Dave, Eve and Floyd are Persons,

$$A \sqsubseteq \text{Person} \wedge B \sqsubseteq \text{Person} \wedge \ldots \wedge F \sqsubseteq \text{Person}$$

Here A, B, C, D, E and F are quasi-nominals. A nominal is a
concept that is satisfied by exactly one individual. In $\mathcal{ALC}$ we
cannot express that a concept is a nominal but we can tacitly
add information like $\neg(A \equiv \bot)$ or $(A \sqcap B) \equiv \bot$, which give us
the desired properties.

- Opol and Persche are Cars and the car in question (TheCar)
is one of them:

$$O \sqsubseteq \text{Car} \wedge P \sqsubseteq \text{Car}, \text{TheCar} \equiv O \vee \text{TheCar} \equiv P$$

(again, O, P are quasi-nominals)

- Any Person is either blond, brunette or red-haired:

$$\text{Red} \sqcup \text{Blond} \sqcup \text{Brunette} \equiv \text{Person} \wedge \text{Red} \sqcap \text{Blond} \equiv \perp \wedge \ldots$$

- The community consists of exactly those persons:

$$\text{Community} \equiv A \sqcup B \sqcup \ldots \sqcup F$$

- The car in question had only one driver, who is from the community:

$$\exists \text{DriverOf.TheCar} \equiv A \vee \ldots \vee \exists \text{DriverOf.TheCar} \equiv F$$

In addition, the policeman knows the hair colour (HairColor) of the driver of the car ($\exists$DriverOf.TheCar), that is

$$\exists \text{DriverOf.TheCar} \sqsubseteq \text{HairColor}$$

where HairColor is exactly one of Blond, Red or Brunette. The policeman also knows the driven car (TheCar), which is either O or P. Hence we have

$$\text{HairColor} \equiv \text{Blond} \wedge \text{TheCar} \equiv O$$

or

$$\text{HairColor} \equiv \text{Red} \wedge \text{TheCar} \equiv P$$

or

$$\ldots$$

Note that we have only one of them but not several simultaneously. We do not fix this knowledge now so that we can discuss several different settings.

To the knowledge of the gardener we add following:

- He knows the hair colours:

$$A, B, C \sqsubseteq \text{Blond}, \ D, E \sqsubseteq \text{Brunette and } F \sqsubseteq \text{Red}$$

  (notice, that e.g. from this and the previously given information $\text{Red} \sqcap \text{Blond} \equiv \bot$ it follows $\neg F \sqsubseteq \text{Blond}$, so the gardener knows the exact hair colour of community members)

- He has seen Alice, Carol and Floyd go to the carport and heard them leave by car:

$$\exists \text{DriverOf.TheCar} \sqsubseteq A \sqcup C \sqcup F$$

- If they took the Persche, certainly Floyd was its driver:

$$\text{TheCar} \equiv P \rightarrow (F \equiv \exists \text{DriverOf}.P \wedge (A \sqcup C) \sqsupseteq \exists \text{DriverOf}.O)$$

  (notice, that $\exists \text{DriverOf}.O \sqsubseteq (A \sqcup C)$ does not mean they actually took the other car, since $\exists \text{DriverOf}.O) \equiv \bot$ could hold.)

Since the gardener does not want one of the group to be fined, he must not give the policeman a chance to infer who drove that car. Hence the secrets are

$$A \equiv \exists \text{DriverOf.TheCar},$$
$$B \equiv \exists \text{DriverOf.TheCar},$$

$$\dots,$$
$$F \equiv \exists\text{DriverOf.TheCar}.$$

So far we do not have a privacy configuration, since $\mathcal{CK} \models \mathcal{AK}$ does not hold. However, once the policeman told (prior to starting his inquiries) the gardener that the community's Persche was photographed by a speed-camera (i.e. TheCar $\equiv P$), and hence the gardener knows

$$F \equiv \exists\text{DriverOf.TheCar}$$

this is achieved, since now also the driver's hair colour (red)

$$\exists\text{DriverOf.TheCar} \sqsubseteq \text{Red}$$

can be inferred by the gardener.

In order to establish a privacy configuration in the situation where the Opol was driven, the policeman has to give out both information:

$$\text{TheCar} \equiv O \quad \text{and} \quad \exists\text{DriverOf.TheCar} \sqsubseteq \text{HairColor}$$

We define two query sequences of the policeman to provide exemplary answers of the presented censor-functions:

$$\mathbf{P}^1 := (\exists\text{DriverOf.TheCar} \equiv A, \exists\text{DriverOf.TheCar} \equiv B,$$
$$\dots, \exists\text{DriverOf.TheCar} \equiv F, t, t, \dots)$$
$$\mathbf{P}^2 := (\exists\text{DriverOf.TheCar} \sqsubseteq \text{HairColor},$$
$$A \sqsubseteq \overline{\text{HairColor}}, B \sqsubseteq \overline{\text{HairColor}}, \dots, F \sqsubseteq \overline{\text{HairColor}}, t, t, \dots)$$

We keep these queries very simple in order to not increase the complexity of this already very long example set-up. The first sequence asks only the hidden secrets, the second only information on the hair-colours.

In order to qualify our gardener as an answering-function (here, the privacy configuration is fixed), he needs to be sure about the knowledge of the policeman. So we assume, he himself has some experience with photographs taken by speeding-cameras and hence knows, that only hair-colours and license-plates are visible on them. To upgrade him to a censor, we would have to make him independent of the observed situation as well. E.g. he would have to be able to react even if no one drove or the policeman had less or more knowledge (as long as all secrets are kept in the start) or even in a completely different start situation (like no knowledge at all).

Example 3.2.5 (Evaluation Censors)
So equipped, our gardener can choose both "strategies" of example 2.4.7: the revealing and the overprotective censor. However neither of these is a good choice. The revealing strategy is trivially no choice, since—so far our assumption—he wants to protect his employers, but would confirm that Floyd drove the car or imply this, e.g. by ruling out all others. So with the trivial censor our gardener would answer (for TheCar $\equiv P$):

$$\mathrm{censor}_{\mathcal{RC}\dots}(\mathbf{P}^1) = (f, f, f, f, f, t, t, t, \dots)$$

$$\mathrm{censor}_{\mathcal{RC}\dots}(\mathbf{P}^2) = (t, t, t, t, t, t, f, t, t, \dots)$$

In both sequences the policeman has the perpetrator after the sixth answer.

With the overprotective approach on the other side, he might raise the policeman's suspicion, since the policeman might conclude (on a meta level) that the gardener must know all details to be able to copy his knowledge. For example, because the gardener "told him" (in our view confirmed) the red hair-colour of the driver (again with TheCar $\equiv P$).

$$\text{censor}_{\mathcal{R}...}(\mathbf{P}^1) = (u, u, u, u, u, u, t, t, \ldots)$$

$$\text{censor}_{\mathcal{R}...}(\mathbf{P}^2) = (t, u, u, u, u, u, u, t, t, \ldots) \qquad \Box$$

Chapter 4

Dependencies on Language Structures

4.1 Handling Negation

In case a semantics possesses a negation, the situation that has to be
This is due to the fact that negative knowledge of a formula can be
replaced by positive knowledge of a negated formula. In this section
we will proof that one can then just use the positive notations of all
defined symbols.

Definition 4.1.1

Let $\psi \in \mathcal{L}$ and $a \in \{t, f, u, r\}$. The (intended) *positive content* (in a semantics with negation) of a as answer to ψ is given by

$$\mathrm{Cont}(\psi, a) = \begin{cases} \{\Box\psi\} & \text{if} \quad a = t \\ \{\Box\neg\psi\} & \text{if} \quad a = f \\ \{\Diamond\psi, \Diamond\neg\psi\} & \text{if} \quad a = u \\ \emptyset & \text{if} \quad a = r \end{cases}$$

(Repeating remark 2.4.12).

Analogously, their *negative content* is given by

$$\mathrm{Cont}(\psi, a) = \begin{cases} \{\blacksquare\neg\psi\} & \text{if} \quad a = t \\ \{\blacksquare\psi\} & \text{if} \quad a = f \\ \{\blacklozenge\psi, \blacklozenge\neg\psi\} & \text{if} \quad a = u \\ \emptyset & \text{if} \quad a = r \end{cases}$$

in the natural way. □

Definition 4.1.2

Let $\mathcal{KK} = (\mathcal{T}, \mathcal{F})$ be a knowledge-base.

Then, the knowledge-base given by

$$\overline{\mathcal{KK}} := (\mathcal{T} \cup \{\neg\psi \mid \psi \in \mathcal{F}\}, \emptyset)$$

is called positive version of $\mathcal{KK}$ and the knowledge-base given by

$$\underline{\mathcal{KK}} := (\emptyset, \mathcal{F} \cup \{\neg\psi \mid \psi \in \mathcal{T}\})$$

is called negative version of $\mathcal{KK}$. □

52

Lemma 4.1.3

Let $\mathcal{KC}$ be a knowledge-base. Then the knowledge-bases $\overline{\mathcal{KC}}$ and $\underline{\mathcal{KC}}$ satisfy the same interpretations as $\mathcal{KC}$. □

PROOF To show $\{i \in \mathcal{I} \mid i \vDash \mathcal{KC}\} = \{i \in \mathcal{I} \mid i \vDash \overline{\mathcal{KC}}\}$:

In case $\mathcal{F}_{\mathcal{KC}} = \emptyset$ this is trivial.

Otherwise let $i \vDash \mathcal{KC}$. By definition, this means $i \vDash \mathcal{T}_{\mathcal{KC}}$ and $i \overset{co}{\vDash} \mathcal{F}_{\mathcal{KC}}$. Hence, for all $\psi \in \mathcal{F}_{\mathcal{KC}}$ it is $i \nvDash \psi$.

Therefore, by remark 2.2.15 it follows that $i \vDash \neg\psi$, resulting in $i \vDash \{\neg\psi \mid \psi \in \mathcal{F}\}$ and hence $i \vDash \overline{\mathcal{KC}}$.

Let $i \vDash \overline{\mathcal{KC}}$. Then, clearly we have $i \vDash \mathcal{T}_{\mathcal{KC}}$ and $i \vDash \neg\psi$ for all $\psi \in \mathcal{F}_{\mathcal{KC}}$. Hence, by definition of the negation operator 2.2.14, we have $i \nvDash \psi$.

Therefore, it holds $i \overset{co}{\vDash} \mathcal{F}_{\mathcal{KC}}$, and hence $i \vDash \mathcal{KC}$.

The equivalence $\{i \in \mathcal{I} \mid i \vDash \mathcal{KC}\} = \{i \in \mathcal{I} \mid i \vDash \overline{\mathcal{KC}}\}$ follows analogously. ■

The following theorem is now immediate:

Theorem 4.1.4

Let censor be any censor on a semantics with negation. If replacing

- *the usual content (defined in 2.4.11) by the positive [negative] content,*

- *and accordingly all knowledge-bases by their positive [negative] versions,*

does not change any of the censor's answers, all quality properties (i.e. continuous, credible, effective, truthful, minimal invasive, [atomic] repudiating) of the censor remain unchanged. □

53

PROOF Continuity follows, because it is completely independent
from the knowledge-bases.

For the other properties: If all answers remain unchanged, so do the
sets of interpretations of the state cloud by lemma 4.1.3. Since also
all evaluations remain unchanged, the claim follows. ∎

4.2 Pseudo-Atomicity and Evaluation

When trying to formalize real situations (e.g. statements in natural
language) as propositional statements, often the following approach
is used. First, more or less independent basic statements are iso-
lated and represented by a propositional letter (atom). Second, the
so separated letters are used to rebuild the original dependencies.
Finally, the thus found formulae form a knowledge-base on which
further reasoning is based.

This approach has several advantages, mainly that it is easy and
straightforward. However, it has the disadvantage that the selection
of the basic statements is usually not unique. Moreover it is not
clear whether dependencies of ignored substatements affect query
evaluation.

In this section we show that the evaluation of known statements
is *not* affected by unknown substatements. Therefore, the typical
modelling approach is indeed safe. Furthermore, the approach still
works on all sorts of subboolean semantics, as long as their basis-
formulae are atomic.

To provide a formal proof of this fact, we define an alternative incomplete evaluator, which is based on the knowledge of the
truth-values of some basis-formulae. We will proceed to show that

this evaluator is immediately usable on atomic knowledge-bases and then adapt the base sets to identify necessary conditions on basis-formulae. With this tools, we are able to prove that in presence of reasonable assumptions, the propositional subformulae of pseudo-atomic elements do indeed not affect the calculations of truth-values and furthermore, that these formulae can be safely assumed to be atomic.

The following lemma can be found in multiple variants in most introductory textbooks to propositional logic:

Lemma 4.2.1

Every Boolean function $b : \{0,1\}^n \to \{0,1\}$ can be expressed as combination of the two Boolean functions $b_\neg(v) = 1 - v$ (negation) and $b_\wedge(v_1, v_2) = \min(v_1, v_2)$ (conjunction).

I.e. for each Boolean function b there is a representation of the function $b' \in \mathbb{B}_n^{\neg,\wedge}$, where the set of Boolean functions of degree n and $\wedge, \neg$ combinations $\mathbb{B}_n^{\neg,\wedge}$ is inductively defined by

- $\pi_i^n \in \mathbb{B}^{\neg,\wedge}$ *(i-th projection)*,
  with $\pi_i(v_1, \ldots, v_n) = v_i$ for all $1 \leq i \leq n$

- *if $t_1, t_2 \in \mathbb{B}^{\neg,\wedge}$ then $b_\wedge \circ (t_1, t_2) \in \mathbb{B}^{\neg,\wedge}$,*
  with the pairing $(t_1, t_2) \notin \mathbb{B}^{\neg,\wedge}$ being defined by

$$(t_1, t_2)(v_1, \ldots, v_n) = (t_1(v_1, \ldots, v_n), t_1(v_1, \ldots, v_n))$$

- *if $t \in \mathbb{B}^{\neg,\wedge}$ then $b_\neg \circ t \in \mathbb{B}^{\neg,\wedge}$*

(the application order by $\circ$ is from right to left), and for all tuples $(v_1, \ldots, v_n) \in \{0,1\}^n$ it holds $b(v_1, \ldots, v_n) = b'(v_1, \ldots, v_n)$. □

Notice that the lemma can be read like this: When viewing the elements of $\mathbb{B}^{\neg,\wedge}$ as functions (and not as representations of functions), the sets $\{b \mid b : \{0,1\}^n \to \{0,1\}\}$ and $\mathbb{B}^{\neg,\wedge}$ are identical. Choosing $\neg$ and $\wedge$ as operators has plainly technical reasons. Mainly that it allows to keep negation (and hence its properties from the previous section). The operator $\wedge$ was chosen, because it allows to push truth "inward", as will be shown below: If a formula $\psi_1 \wedge \psi_2$ is true, so are ψ_1 and ψ_2. This will be used to reduce evaluation overhead by storing formulae that are as short as possible in the knowledge-base. Of course the arguments in this section could be similarly done by using $\vee$ (disjunction) and hence pushing falsity inward.

Example 4.2.2

The constant Boolean function

$$b(v_1, \ldots, v_n) = 1$$

could be calculated by

$$b(v_1, \ldots, v_n) = 1 - \min(1 - v_1, v_1)$$

and hence could be represented by

$$b' = b_\neg \circ b_\wedge \circ (b_\neg \circ \pi_1, \pi_1)$$

This representation is obviously not unique. $\qquad\square$

Definition 4.2.3 (Boolean Completion)

Let $\mathcal{S} = (\mathcal{L}, \mathfrak{I}, \vDash)$ be a subboolean semantics with base formulae $\mathfrak{B}$ and operators $\mathfrak{D}$. Then the *Boolean completion* $\mathcal{S}^\star = (\mathcal{L}^\star, \mathfrak{I}^\star, \vDash^\star)$ is defined as follows:

- $\mathcal{L}^*$ is defined by all words derived by φ in the Backus–Naur form

$$\varphi ::= b \mathop{|}_{b \in \mathfrak{B}} \mid (\neg\varphi) \mid (\varphi \wedge \varphi)$$

where $\neg$, $\wedge$ are new symbols and hence do not appear in $\mathcal{L}$,

- $\mathfrak{I}^* := \{(\mathcal{T}, \mathcal{F}) \mid \mathcal{T} \cup \mathcal{F} = \mathfrak{B}$ and $\mathcal{T} \cap \mathcal{F} = \emptyset\}$ is the set of binary partitions of $\mathfrak{B}$, and

- $(\mathcal{T}, \mathcal{F}) \vDash^* \psi$ is inductively defined by

  – For $\psi \in \mathfrak{B}$:

  $$\psi \in \mathcal{T} \text{ iff } (\mathcal{T}, \mathcal{F}) \vDash^* \psi$$

  – For $\psi = \neg\psi'$:

  $$(\mathcal{T}, \mathcal{F}) \vDash^* \psi \text{ iff } (\mathcal{T}, \mathcal{F}) \nvDash^* \psi'$$

  – For $\psi = \psi_1 \wedge \psi_2$:

  $$(\mathcal{T}, \mathcal{F}) \vDash^* \psi \text{ iff } (\mathcal{T}, \mathcal{F}) \vDash^* \psi_1 \text{ and } (\mathcal{T}, \mathcal{F}) \vDash^* \psi_2$$

In addition, the *length* $\#\psi$ of a $\mathcal{L}^*$ formula is defined to be the number of logical connectors ($\neg$, $\wedge$) in the formula. □

Example 4.2.4

Propositional logic is its own Boolean completion, i.e. $\mathbb{P}_A = \mathbb{P}_A^\star$ □

Remark 4.2.5

It is worth noticing, that the extension of $\vDash^*$ to satisfaction and co-satisfaction of sets of formulae, defined in 2.2.4, or to knowledge-bases, defined in 2.2.3, does not cause ambiguity problems. In definition 4.2.3 the pair $(\mathcal{T}, \mathcal{F}) \in \mathfrak{I}^*$ refers to a specific interpretation.

However, if $(\mathcal{T},\mathcal{F})$ refers to a knowledge-base over $\mathcal{S}^\star$, the same
formulae are satisfied or co-satisfied. Especially, the semantical im-
plications

- $(\mathcal{T},\mathcal{F}) \vDash^\star (\mathcal{T},\mathcal{F})$

- $(\mathcal{T},\mathcal{F}) \vDash^\star \mathcal{T}$

- $(\mathcal{T},\mathcal{F}) \overset{co}{\vDash^\star} \mathcal{F}$

hold in all defined meanings. □

Definition 4.2.6 (Boolean Embedding)
Let $\mathcal{S} = (\mathcal{L},\mathfrak{I},\vDash)$ be a subboolean semantics with base formulae $\mathfrak{B}$
and operators $\mathfrak{O}$ and let $\mathcal{S}^\star = (\mathcal{L}^\star,\mathfrak{I}^\star,\vDash^\star)$ its Boolean completion.

Then the embedding $\star : \mathcal{L} \to \mathcal{L}^\star$ as defined as follows is called
Boolean embedding.

For each operator $o(\psi_1,\ldots,\psi_{\deg o}) \in \mathfrak{O}$ fix an equivalent representation b'_o of b_o via lemma 4.2.1 consisting of combinations of $b_\neg$
and $b_\wedge$.

The embedding $\star : \mathcal{L} \to \mathcal{L}^\star$ is inductively defined as follows:

- If $\psi \in \mathfrak{B}$:

$$\star(\psi) = \psi$$

- If $\psi = o(\psi_1,\ldots,\psi_{\deg(o)})$:

$$\star(\psi) = I(b'_o)$$

and I is inductively defined as follows:

- $I(\pi_i^{\deg(o)}) = \star(\psi_i)$

58

$$- \ I(b_\neg \circ t) = (\neg I(t))$$

$$- \ I(b_\wedge \circ (t_1, t_2)) = (I(t_1) \wedge I(t_2))$$

(The function I provides a transformation of the Boolean functions into $\mathcal{L}^*$ formulae. Obviously, it depends as well on the subformulae $\psi_1, \ldots, \psi_{\deg(o)}$, which we omitted from the formula's signature for simplification). □

Let us point out, that $\star$ is in general not deterministic (and hence not a function), since there might be several ways to construct a formula from the base-formulae by means of the operators.

Example 4.2.7
Assume a semantic $\mathcal{S}$ with language $\mathcal{L} = \{x, y\}$ with $y \in \mathcal{T}_{\mathcal{S}}$, the constant operator $o : \mathcal{L} \to \mathcal{L}$ with

$$o(x) = o(y) = y$$

has the constant Boolean function $b_o = 1$, which has the represenatiation

$$b' = b_\neg \circ b_\wedge \circ (b_\neg \circ \pi_1, \pi_1)$$

seen in example 4.2.2. A possible basis is $\mathfrak{B} := \{a\}$.
As translation $\star(b)$ only $\star(o(a))$ can be used, which is calculated to be

$$\star(b) = \neg(\neg a \wedge a)$$ □

59

Lemma 4.2.8

Let $S = (\mathcal{L}, \mathfrak{I}, \vDash)$ be a subboolean semantics with base formulae $\mathfrak{B}$ and operators $\mathfrak{O}$, let $S^* = (\mathcal{L}^*, \mathfrak{I}^*, \vDash^*)$ its Boolean completion and let $\star$ be their Boolean embedding.

Then $\star$ is a function, iff all combined formulae $\psi \in \mathcal{L} \backslash \mathfrak{B}$ are uniquely expressible by base formulae and operators.

If additionally S is atomic, then

1. the satisfaction of embedded formulae is independent of the choice of the operator representations, i.e. for two embeddings $\star_1$ and $\star_2$ and all formulae $\psi \in \mathcal{L}$ it holds

$$(\mathcal{T}, \mathcal{F}) \vDash^* \star_1(\psi) \text{ iff } (\mathcal{T}, \mathcal{F}) \vDash^* \star_2(\psi),$$

2. and all formulae $\psi \in \mathcal{L}$ are semantically implied by an atomic knowledge-base $(\mathcal{T}, \mathcal{F})$ over S iff they are satisfied in the interpretation $(\mathcal{T}, \mathcal{F})$ of S^*, i.e. for all $\psi \in \mathcal{L}$ and $\mathcal{T}, \mathcal{F} \subseteq \mathfrak{B}$ it holds

$$(\mathcal{T}, \mathcal{F}) \vDash \psi \text{ iff } (\mathcal{T}, \mathcal{F}) \vDash^* \star(\psi). \qquad \square$$

PROOF The first part of the lemma is trivial, since it is just a substitution of operators.

For the second part it suffices to show claim 2. Claim 1 then follows by definition of being subboolean (2.2.9) and observing that satisfaction of the formulae $\star(\psi)$ is only dependent on the satisfaction of base formulae and the Boolean function. Its representation does not matter.

Claim 2 is shown by induction on the structure of $\mathcal{L}$:

- If $\psi \in \mathfrak{B}$ is a base formula:

  Assume $(\mathcal{T}, \mathcal{F}) \vDash \psi$. Then there are three cases:

  - $\psi \in \mathcal{T}$:

    If $(\mathcal{T}, \mathcal{F})$ is not satisfiable, this follows as in the next case. Otherwise, by atomicity $\mathcal{T} \cap \mathcal{F} = \emptyset$ and all interpretations $(\mathcal{T}', \mathcal{F}') \in \mathfrak{I}^\star$, with $(\mathcal{T}', \mathcal{F}') \vDash^\star (\mathcal{T}, \mathcal{F})$, satisfy $\mathcal{T} \subseteq \mathcal{T}'$ and $\mathcal{F} \subseteq \mathcal{F}'$. Hence $\psi = \star(\psi) \in \mathcal{T}'$ and $(\mathcal{T}', \mathcal{F}') \vDash^\star \star(\psi)$.

  - $\psi \in \mathcal{F}$:

    Then, no interpretation $i \in \mathfrak{I}$ satisfies $(\mathcal{T}, \mathcal{F})$, since this would simultaneously imply $i \vDash \psi$ and $i \nvDash \psi$.

    However, by atomicity, this implies that there is a base formula $\varphi \in \mathcal{T} \cap \mathcal{F}$. Hence, there is no interpretation $(\mathcal{T}', \mathcal{F}') \in \mathfrak{I}^\star$, that satisfies $(\mathcal{T}', \mathcal{F}') \vDash^\star (\mathcal{T}, \mathcal{F})$, since φ would have to be an element of both $\mathcal{T}'$ and $\mathcal{F}'$, in violation of $(\mathcal{T}', \mathcal{F}')$ being a partition.

  - $\psi \in \mathfrak{B} \setminus (\mathcal{T} \cup \mathcal{F})$:

    Then, by atomicity, there is an interpretation $i \in \mathfrak{I}$, s.t.

    $$i \in \{j \in \mathfrak{I} \mid j \vDash \mathcal{T}\} \cap \{j \in \mathfrak{I} \mid j \overset{co}{\vDash} \{\psi\}\}$$

    in violation of the assumption $(\mathcal{T}, \mathcal{F}) \vDash \psi$.

The case $(\mathcal{T}, \mathcal{F}) \nvDash \psi$ follows analogously.

- if $\psi = o(\psi_1, \ldots \psi_{\deg(o)})$:

  By induction hypothesis, we have for all $1 \leq i \leq \deg(o)$

$$(\mathcal{T}, \mathcal{F}) \models \psi_i \text{ iff } (\mathcal{T}, \mathcal{F}) \models^\star \star(\psi_i).$$

The claim follows by the definition of being subboolean. ∎

Remark 4.2.9

It is worth noticing, that in the above lemma 4.2.8, the identity

$$(\mathcal{T}, \mathcal{F}) \models \psi \text{ iff } (\mathcal{T}, \mathcal{F}) \models^\star \star(\psi)$$

holds indeed for all subsets $\mathcal{T}, \mathcal{F} \subseteq \mathfrak{B}$ and hence, $(\mathcal{T}, \mathcal{F})$ is not (necessarily) a partitions of $\mathfrak{B}$. Thus, on the right side the semantic implication is by an atomic knowledge-base (of $\mathcal{L}^\star$) and not (necessarily) by an interpretation (in $\mathfrak{I}^\star$). □

Definition 4.2.10 ((Pseudo-)Atomic Evaluator)

Let $\mathcal{S} = (\mathcal{L}, \mathfrak{I}, \models)$ be an atomic semantics with base formulae $\mathfrak{B}$ and $\mathcal{S}^\star = (\mathcal{L}^\star, \mathfrak{I}^\star, \models^\star)$ be its structured completion. Furthermore, let $\mathcal{T}_{\mathcal{S}^\star}$ denote the tautologies and $\mathcal{F}_{\mathcal{S}^\star}$ the unsatisfiables of $\mathcal{S}^\star$ (compare definition 2.2.7). Furthermore, let $\mathcal{T}, \mathcal{F} \subseteq \mathcal{L}^\star \setminus (\mathcal{T}_{\mathcal{S}^\star} \cup \mathcal{F}_{\mathcal{S}^\star})$.

The *atomic evaluator* $\mathsf{eval}^a_{(\mathcal{T}, \mathcal{F})}$ of $\mathcal{S}^\star$ is defined on formulae of $\mathcal{L}^\star$ by

- If $\psi \in \mathcal{T} \cup \mathcal{F} \cup \mathfrak{B} \cup \mathcal{T}_{\mathcal{S}^\star} \cup \mathcal{F}_{\mathcal{S}^\star}$, then

$$\mathsf{eval}^a_{(\mathcal{T}, \mathcal{F})}(\psi) = \begin{cases} t & \psi \in \mathcal{T} \cup \mathcal{T}_{\mathcal{S}^\star} \\ f & \psi \in (\mathcal{F} \cup \mathcal{F}_{\mathcal{S}^\star}) \setminus \mathcal{T} \\ u & \text{else (i.e. } \psi \in \mathfrak{B} \setminus (\mathcal{T} \cup \mathcal{F})) \end{cases}$$

- Otherwise we make a case distinction on the outermost connective of ψ

  - if $\psi = \neg\psi'$ then

  $$\mathsf{eval}^a_{(\mathcal{T},\mathcal{F})}(\psi) = \begin{cases} t & \mathsf{eval}^a_{(\mathcal{T},\mathcal{F})}(\psi') = f \\ f & \mathsf{eval}^a_{(\mathcal{T},\mathcal{F})}(\psi') = t \\ u & \text{else} \end{cases}$$

  - and if $\psi = \psi_1 \wedge \psi_2$, then

  $$\mathsf{eval}^a_{(\mathcal{T},\mathcal{F})}(\psi) = \begin{cases} t & \text{iff.} & \mathsf{eval}^a_{(\mathcal{T},\mathcal{F})}(\psi_1) = t \text{ and} \\ & & \mathsf{eval}^a_{(\mathcal{T},\mathcal{F})}(\psi_2) = t \\ f & \text{iff.} & \mathsf{eval}^a_{(\mathcal{T},\mathcal{F})}(\psi_1) = f \text{ or} \\ & & \mathsf{eval}^a_{(\mathcal{T},\mathcal{F})}(\psi_2) = f \\ u & \text{else} \end{cases}$$

  $\square$

Lemma 4.2.11

In the situation of definition 4.2.10, the incomplete evaluator (definition 2.3.1) of $\mathcal{S}^\star$ is equivalent to the atomic evaluator of $\mathcal{S}^\star$ for consistent knowledge-bases. I.e. if $(\mathcal{T},\mathcal{F})$ is a consistent, atomic knowledge-base on $\mathcal{S}^\star$, then it holds

$$\mathsf{eval}^a_{(\mathcal{T},\mathcal{F})}(\psi) = \mathsf{eval}_{(\mathcal{T},\mathcal{F})}(\psi)$$

on all $\psi \in \mathcal{L}^\star$. $\square$

PROOF It is to prove that each formula gets assigned the same truth value in either case of calculation.

We proceed by induction on the structure of the formulae.

Base case:

For all atoms $a \in \mathfrak{B}$: By remark 2.2.11, $a \notin \mathcal{T}_{\mathcal{S}^*} \cup \mathcal{F}_{\mathcal{S}^*}$. Hence, by atomicity and consistency of $(\mathcal{T}, \mathcal{F})$ this case is obvious.

Induction step:

For simplicity we will only write $(\mathcal{T}_\mathsf{A}, \mathcal{F}_\mathsf{A})$ for all partitions of $\mathfrak{B}$, that satisfy $(\mathcal{T}_\mathsf{A}, \mathcal{F}_\mathsf{A}) \vDash^* (\mathcal{T}, \mathcal{F})$.

By atomicity, those are exactly the partitions satisfying $\mathcal{T} \subseteq \mathcal{T}_\mathsf{A}$ and $\mathcal{F} \subseteq \mathcal{F}_\mathsf{A}$.

Case $\psi = \neg \psi'$.

This case is obvious.

Case $\psi := \psi_1 \wedge \psi_2$. We distinguish the following cases:

- Assume $\mathrm{eval}_{(\mathcal{T},\mathcal{F})}(\psi) = t$.

  In case $\psi \in \mathcal{T}_{\mathcal{S}^*}$, $\mathrm{eval}^a_{(\mathcal{T},\mathcal{F})}(\psi) = t$ follows immediately. Otherwise by definition, $\mathrm{eval}_{(\mathcal{T},\mathcal{F})}(\psi) = t$ holds if and only if in all partitions $(\mathcal{T}_\mathsf{A}, \mathcal{F}_\mathsf{A})$ we have $(\mathcal{T}_\mathsf{A}, \mathcal{F}_\mathsf{A}) \vDash^* \psi$, which means, by definition of $\vDash^*$, that $(\mathcal{T}_\mathsf{A}, \mathcal{F}_\mathsf{A}) \vDash^* \{\psi_1, \psi_2\}$.

  Hence $\mathrm{eval}_{(\mathcal{T},\mathcal{F})}(\psi_1) = t$ and $\mathrm{eval}_{(\mathcal{T},\mathcal{F})}(\psi_2) = t$ and the case follows by IH. and the definition of $\mathrm{eval}^a_{(\mathcal{T},\mathcal{F})}$.

- Assume $\mathrm{eval}_{(\mathcal{T},\mathcal{F})}(\psi) = f$.

  In case $\psi \in \mathcal{F}_{\mathcal{S}^*}$, $\mathrm{eval}^a_{(\mathcal{T},\mathcal{F})}(\psi) = f$ follows immediately. Otherwise there is a partition $(\mathcal{T}_\mathsf{A}, \mathcal{F}_\mathsf{A})$, such that $(\mathcal{T}_\mathsf{A}, \mathcal{F}_\mathsf{A}) \vDash^* \psi$ (therefore $\psi \notin \mathcal{T}_{\mathcal{S}^*}$), hence

$$\text{not } (\mathcal{T}_\mathsf{A}, \mathcal{F}_\mathsf{A}) \vDash^* \psi_1 \text{ or not } (\mathcal{T}_\mathsf{A}, \mathcal{F}_\mathsf{A}) \vDash^* \psi_2.$$

64

We assume wlog that not $(\mathcal{T}_{\!A}, \mathcal{F}_{\!A}) \models^{\star} \psi_1$: By IH. we get $\mathrm{eval}^a_{(\mathcal{T},\mathcal{F})}(\psi_1) = f$ and hence by construction $\mathrm{eval}^a_{(\mathcal{T},\mathcal{F})}(\psi) = f$.

- Assume $\mathrm{eval}_{(\mathcal{T},\mathcal{F})}(\psi) = u$.
  Then there are partitions $(\mathcal{T}_{\!A}, \mathcal{F}_{\!A}) \models^{\star} \psi$ and $(\mathcal{T}_{\!A}', \mathcal{F}_{\!A}') \not\models^{\star} \psi$,
  hence $\psi \notin \mathcal{T}_{\!S^\star}$ and $\psi \notin \mathcal{F}_{\!S^\star}$.
  Also (at least) one of $(\mathcal{T}_{\!A}', \mathcal{F}_{\!A}') \not\models^{\star} \psi_1$ or $(\mathcal{T}_{\!A}', \mathcal{F}_{\!A}') \not\models^{\star} \psi_2$ holds.
  Assume wlog the first.
  Hence $\mathrm{eval}_{(\mathcal{T},\mathcal{F})}(\psi_1) = u$ and $\mathrm{eval}_{(\mathcal{T},\mathcal{F})}(\psi_2) \in \{t, u\}$. By IH. and construction follows $\mathrm{eval}^a_{(\mathcal{T},\mathcal{F})}(\psi) = u$

The other directions follow by reversing the arguments. ∎

Remark 4.2.12

Notice, that there are two critical checks above:

First, that subformulae evaluating to u do not directly affect the calculation of the total value. Indeed the only direct check on being unknown is done in the case of base formulae. Second, that we need to deal with tautologies and unsatisfiables. Especially this check must be executed prior to the calculation on subformulae, since the three cases in the build up of the evaluator are not structuredly distinct. □

Combining lemmata 4.2.11 and 4.2.8 the following corollary follows immediately:

Corollary 4.2.13

In the situation of definition 4.2.10, and using the structured embedding $\star$. *It holds for all consistent atomic knowledge-bases* $(\mathcal{T}, \mathcal{F})$ *of* $\mathcal{S}$, *that*

$$\mathrm{eval}_{(\mathcal{T},\mathcal{F})}(\psi) = \mathrm{eval}^a_{(\mathcal{T},\mathcal{F})}(\star(\psi))$$

for all $\psi \in \mathcal{L}$. (The left evaluation is determined on $\mathcal{S}$, but the right evaluation on $\mathcal{S}^\star$.) □

Lemma 4.2.14

In the situation of definition 4.2.10, let $(\mathcal{T}, \mathcal{F})$ be a consistent knowledge-base of $\mathcal{S}$ (not necessarily atomic).

Furthermore define a knowledge-base $(\mathcal{T}^\star, \mathcal{F}^\star)$ by

- $\mathcal{T}^\star := \{\star(\psi) \in \mathcal{L}^\star \mid \psi \in \mathcal{T}\}$

- $\mathcal{F}^\star := \{\star(\psi) \in \mathcal{L}^\star \mid \psi \in \mathcal{F}\}$

Then there exist unique subsets

- $\mathcal{T}^a \subseteq \{\psi \in \mathcal{L}^\star \mid \mathsf{eval}_{(\mathcal{T}^\star, \mathcal{F}^\star)}(\psi) = t\} \setminus \mathcal{T}_{\mathcal{S}^\star}$ *and*

- $\mathcal{F}^a \subseteq \{\psi \in \mathcal{L}^\star \mid \mathsf{eval}_{(\mathcal{T}^\star, \mathcal{F}^\star)}(\psi) = f\} \setminus \mathcal{F}_{\mathcal{S}^\star}$

that satisfy the following conditions: for all $\psi, \psi_1, \psi_2 \in \mathcal{L}^\star$

> *p1)* $\mathsf{eval}^a_{(\mathcal{T}^a, \mathcal{F}^a)}(\psi) = \mathsf{eval}_{(\mathcal{T}^\star, \mathcal{F}^\star)}(\psi),$

> *p2)* $\neg\psi \notin \mathcal{T}^a \cup \mathcal{F}^a$
>
> *(formulae are free of negation prefixes)*

> *p3) if $\psi_1 \wedge \psi_2 \in \mathcal{T}^a \cup \mathcal{F}^a$,*
>
> *then $\mathsf{eval}_{(\mathcal{T}^\star, \mathcal{F}^\star)}(\psi_1) = u$ and $\mathsf{eval}_{(\mathcal{T}^\star, \mathcal{F}^\star)}(\psi_2) = u$*
>
> *(all subformulae are unknown).*

Moreover, it holds $\mathcal{T}^a \subseteq \mathfrak{B}$. □

PROOF The existence of subsets with the two minimality properties p2) and p3) is obvious since both just filter out undesired formulae. To proof the equality of $\mathsf{eval}^a_{(\mathcal{T}^a, \mathcal{F}^a)}$ and $\mathsf{eval}_{(\mathcal{T}^\star, \mathcal{F}^\star)}$ we assume that

$$\mathsf{eval}^a_{(\mathcal{T}^a, \mathcal{F}^a)} \neq \mathsf{eval}_{(\mathcal{T}^\star, \mathcal{F}^\star)}$$

and let $\psi \in \mathcal{L}^{\star}$ be a shortest witness. That is

- $\mathsf{eval}^{a}_{(\mathcal{T}^{a}, \mathcal{F}^{a})}(\psi) \neq \mathsf{eval}_{(\mathcal{T}^{\star}, \mathcal{F}^{\star})}(\psi)$ and

- $\mathsf{eval}^{a}_{(\mathcal{T}^{a}, \mathcal{F}^{a})}(\psi') \neq \mathsf{eval}_{(\mathcal{T}^{\star}, \mathcal{F}^{\star})}(\psi')$ implies $\#\psi' \geq \#\psi$.

Obviously, by definitions of $\mathcal{T}_{\mathcal{S}^{\star}}$, $\mathcal{F}_{\mathcal{S}^{\star}}$ and $\mathsf{eval}^{a}_{(\mathcal{T}^{a}, \mathcal{F}^{a})}$, it is

$$\psi \notin \mathcal{T}_{\mathcal{S}^{\star}} \cup \mathcal{F}_{\mathcal{S}^{\star}}.$$

We distinguish all possibilities for $\mathsf{eval}_{(\mathcal{T}^{\star}, \mathcal{F}^{\star})}(\psi)$ depending on the outermost connective of ψ and show that in all cases

$$\mathsf{eval}^{a}_{(\mathcal{T}^{a}, \mathcal{F}^{a})}(\psi) = \mathsf{eval}_{(\mathcal{T}^{\star}, \mathcal{F}^{\star})}(\psi)$$

holds, contradicting our assumptions.

- Assume $\mathsf{eval}_{(\mathcal{T}^{\star}, \mathcal{F}^{\star})}(\psi) = t$.

  - If $\psi \in \mathfrak{B}$: obviously, then $\psi \in \mathcal{T}^{a}$ and hence, by definition of the atomic evaluator $\mathsf{eval}^{a}_{(\mathcal{T}^{a}, \mathcal{F}^{a})}(\psi) = t$.

  - If $\psi = \neg\psi'$: then $f = \mathsf{eval}_{(\mathcal{T}^{\star}, \mathcal{F}^{\star})}(\psi') = \mathsf{eval}^{a}_{(\mathcal{T}^{a}, \mathcal{F}^{a})}(\psi')$, the first equality by definition of $\mathsf{eval}_{(\mathcal{T}^{\star}, \mathcal{F}^{\star})}$ and the second because $\#\psi' < \#\psi$.
  Since ψ starts with a negation, it is $\psi \notin \mathcal{T}^{a} \cup \mathcal{F}^{a}$.
  Hence, since we already ruled out, that ψ is a tautology, it is $\mathsf{eval}^{a}_{(\mathcal{T}^{a}, \mathcal{F}^{a})}(\psi) = t$, as a result of the negation calculation in the definition of $\mathsf{eval}^{a}_{(\mathcal{T}^{a}, \mathcal{F}^{a})}$.

  - If $\psi = \psi_1 \wedge \psi_2$: then by definition

$$\mathsf{eval}_{(\mathcal{T}^{\star}, \mathcal{F}^{\star})}(\psi_1) = \mathsf{eval}_{(\mathcal{T}^{\star}, \mathcal{F}^{\star})}(\psi_2)$$
$$= \mathsf{eval}^{a}_{(\mathcal{T}^{a}, \mathcal{F}^{a})}(\psi_1)$$
$$= \mathsf{eval}^{a}_{(\mathcal{T}^{a}, \mathcal{F}^{a})}(\psi_2) = t.$$

It follows, that $\psi \notin \mathcal{T}^a$.

Obviously, we have $\psi \notin \mathcal{F}^a$ as well, since

$$\text{eval}_{(\mathcal{T}^*, \mathcal{F}^*)}(\psi) \neq f$$

by definition.

Hence the value of $\text{eval}^a_{(\mathcal{T}^a, \mathcal{F}^a)}(\psi) = t$.

- Assume $\text{eval}_{(\mathcal{T}^*, \mathcal{F}^*)}(\psi) = f$:

    - If $\psi \in \mathfrak{B}$: as above.

    - If $\psi = \neg \psi'$: as above

    - If $\psi = \psi_1 \wedge \psi_2$: we distinguish the following cases.
      If $\text{eval}_{(\mathcal{T}^*, \mathcal{F}^*)}(\psi_1) = f$ or $\text{eval}_{(\mathcal{T}^*, \mathcal{F}^*)}(\psi_2) = f$,
      then $\psi \notin \mathcal{F}^a$, and, by reasoning analogous to above, it is

      $$\text{eval}^a_{(\mathcal{T}^a, \mathcal{F}^a)}(\psi) = f.$$

      If $\text{eval}_{(\mathcal{T}^*, \mathcal{F}^*)}(\psi_1) = t$, then $\text{eval}_{(\mathcal{T}^*, \mathcal{F}^*)}(\psi_2) = f$, and
      hence, the previous case applies.
      Analogously for $\text{eval}_{(\mathcal{T}^*, \mathcal{F}^*)}(\psi_2) = t$.
      If $\text{eval}_{(\mathcal{T}^*, \mathcal{F}^*)}(\psi_1) = \text{eval}_{(\mathcal{T}^*, \mathcal{F}^*)}(\psi_2) = u$:
      Then $\psi \in \mathcal{F}^a$ and the desired $\text{eval}^a_{(\mathcal{T}^a, \mathcal{F}^a)}(\psi) = f$ follows
      from the base-case in the definition of the atomic evaluator.

- Assume $\text{eval}_{(\mathcal{T}^*, \mathcal{F}^*)}(\psi) = u$:
  it immediately follows that neither $\text{eval}_{(\mathcal{T}^*, \mathcal{F}^*)}(\psi) = t$ nor
  $\text{eval}_{(\mathcal{T}^*, \mathcal{F}^*)}(\psi) = f$ and hence $\psi \notin \mathcal{T}^a \cup \mathcal{F}^a$.
  Again we distinguish:

    - If $\psi \in \mathfrak{B}$, then $\text{eval}^a_{(\mathcal{T}^a, \mathcal{F}^a)}(\psi) = u$ is immediate.

- If $\psi = \neg\psi'$: This follows exactly as in the above cases.

- If $\psi = \psi_1 \wedge \psi_2$: Then at least one of ψ_1, ψ_2 evaluates to u as well, wlog. $\mathsf{eval}_{(\mathcal{T}^*, \mathcal{F}^*)}(\psi_1) = u$. Also neither can evaluate to f. Hence since $\psi \notin \mathcal{T}^a \cup \mathcal{F}^a$, we have $\mathsf{eval}^a_{(\mathcal{T}^a, \mathcal{F}^a)}(\psi) = u$.

The last claim $\mathcal{T}^a \subseteq \mathfrak{B}$ follows by the two properties p2) and p3) and observing that $\mathsf{eval}^a_{(\mathcal{T}^a, \mathcal{F}^a)}(\psi_1 \wedge \psi_2) = t$ always implies

$$\mathsf{eval}^a_{(\mathcal{T}^a, \mathcal{F}^a)}(\psi_1) = \mathsf{eval}^a_{(\mathcal{T}^a, \mathcal{F}^a)}(\psi_2) = t.$$

Hence, no compund formula can be in $\mathcal{T}^a$. ∎

Definition 4.2.15

The knowledge-base $(\mathcal{T}^a, \mathcal{F}^a)$ (of $\mathcal{S}^*$) found in the previous lemma is called pseudo-atomic version of the knowledge-base $(\mathcal{T}, \mathcal{F})$ (of $\mathcal{S}$). □

Summing up the presented lemmata in this section, it was proven:

Theorem 4.2.16

Let $\mathcal{S} = (\mathcal{L}, \mathfrak{I}, \vDash)$ be an atomic semantics with Boolean completion $\mathcal{S}^*$ and structured embedding $\star$. Furthermore let $(\mathcal{T}, \mathcal{F})$ be a consistent $\mathcal{S}$-knowledge-base. Then it holds

$$\mathsf{eval}_{(\mathcal{T}, \mathcal{F})}(\psi) = \mathsf{eval}^a_{(\mathcal{T}^a, \mathcal{F}^a)}(\star(\psi))$$

for all formulae $\psi \in \mathcal{L}$. □

Chapter 5

Generalized Censors

In this chapter, we discuss various censors that work on all general semantics, as well as restrictions and obstacles that arise from quality restriction. We start by proving some general properties, that are handsome tools in proving desired attributes of censors. Starting with some purely technical tools, as first major consequence will arise, that truthful censors are always credible. The second major consequence is, that in the (non-atomic) general semantics an answer of *unknown* (u) is strong enough to allow very simple lying censors in comparison to the censors found in settings of atomic propositional logic (like [BW08]).

Afterwards we will define and discuss two classes of censors, namely truthful and cooperative lying censors. Since the later ones turn out to have all the desired properties, uncooperative lying censors can not add additional features, and hence there is no need to discuss them.

Finally, we use this chapter to show that indeed all of the presented quality properties are independent. To this end, we will give examples of censors for each configuration.

5.1 Basic Properties

Lemma 5.1.1 (Quartum non datur)

Let $\psi \in \mathcal{L}_{\mathcal{ALC}}$ and let $\mathfrak{C}$ be a $\mathcal{CALC}$-cloud. Then exactly one of the following statements holds:

- $\mathfrak{C} \models \{\Box\psi\}$

- $\mathfrak{C} \models \{\blacksquare\psi\}$

- $\mathfrak{C} \models \{\Diamond\psi, \blacklozenge\neg\psi\}$ □

PROOF Trivial. ∎

Lemma 5.1.2

Let censor be a credible and effective censor, $n \in \mathbb{N}$,

- $\mathcal{F} := \{\psi \mid \blacksquare\psi \in \mathscr{H}_{\mathcal{PC},\mathbf{q}}(n)\}$ and

- $\mathcal{T} := \{\psi \mid \Box\psi \in \mathscr{H}_{\mathcal{PC},\mathbf{q}}(n)\}$

for a fixed privacy configuration $\mathcal{PC} = (\mathcal{CK}, \mathcal{AK}, \mathcal{SK})$, then the following hold:

a) $(\mathcal{T}, \mathcal{F})$ is satisfiable.

b1) $\mathsf{eval}_{(\mathcal{T},\mathcal{F})}(\psi) \in \{u, f\}$ for each $\psi \in \mathcal{T}_{\mathcal{SK}}$

b2) $\mathsf{eval}_{(\mathcal{T},\mathcal{F})}(\psi) \in \{u, t\}$ for each $\psi \in \mathcal{F}_{\mathcal{SK}}$

c1) $\mathsf{eval}_{(\mathcal{T},\mathcal{F})}(\psi) = t$ *if* $\Box\psi \in \mathscr{HC}_{\mathcal{RC},\mathbf{q}}(n)$

c2) $\mathsf{eval}_{(\mathcal{T},\mathcal{F})}(\psi) = f$ *if* $\blacksquare\psi \in \mathscr{HC}_{\mathcal{RC},\mathbf{q}}(n)$

d) $\mathsf{eval}_{(\mathcal{T},\mathcal{F})}(\psi) = u$ *if* $\Diamond\psi \in \mathscr{HC}_{\mathcal{RC},\mathbf{q}}(n)$ *(or if* $\blacklozenge\psi \in \mathscr{HC}_{\mathcal{RC},\mathbf{q}}(n)$*)* □

PROOF Ad a): Since $\mathsf{censor}_{\mathcal{RC}}$ is credible, there is a cloud-model (W, ι) of $\mathscr{HC}_{\mathcal{RC},\mathbf{q}}(n)$. For $w \in W$ by definition $\iota(w)$ satisfies $\mathcal{T}$ and co-satisfies $\mathcal{F}$.

Ad b): Since $\{\Box\psi \mid \psi \in \mathcal{T}\} \cup \{\blacksquare\psi \mid \psi \in \mathcal{F}\} \subseteq \mathscr{HC}_{\mathcal{RC},\mathbf{q}}(n)$ this follows by definition of effectiveness.

Ad c1): By definition of satisfiability ψ must be semantically implied by $\mathcal{T}$, hence by definition of eval the statement follows. c2) follows analogously.

Ad d): By construction of $\mathscr{HC}_{\mathcal{RC},\mathbf{q}}(n)$ from Cont whenever $\Diamond\psi$ or $\blacklozenge\psi$ is contained in $\mathscr{HC}_{\mathcal{RC},\mathbf{q}}(n)$, the other one is included as well. Hence by credibility, in the cloud-model (W, ι) of $\mathscr{HC}_{\mathcal{RC},\mathbf{q}}(n)$, there are worlds $w_1, w_2 \in W$, such that $\iota(w_1) \vDash \psi$ and $\iota(w_2) \vDash \neg\psi$. As in a) $\iota(w_1)$ and $\iota(w_2)$ are models of $(\mathcal{T}, \mathcal{F})$. Hence ψ is neither semantically implied nor semantically co-implied by $(\mathcal{T}, \mathcal{F})$. By definition of eval follows the proposition. ∎

5.1.1 Cloud Translation

There is a slightly less intuitive characterisation of truthful censors via the following translation, which we use to show that every truthful censor is credible:

Definition 5.1.3 (Cloud-Translation)

Let $\mathcal{KK} \subseteq \mathcal{L}$ be a knowledge-base. Then the set

$$\mathrm{ClTr}(\mathcal{KK}) := \bigcup_{\psi \in \mathcal{L}} \mathrm{Cont}(\psi, \mathrm{eval}_{\mathcal{KK}}(\psi))$$

is called (universal) *cloud translation* of $\mathcal{KK}$. □

Some facts are immediate:

Proposition 5.1.4 (Properties)

Let $\mathcal{KK}$ be an arbitrary knowledge-base, let $\psi \in \mathcal{L}$ and let $\mathfrak{C}$ be a $\mathcal{S}$-cloud. The following statements hold

- *If $\mathfrak{C} \models \mathrm{ClTr}(\mathcal{KK})$, then $\mathfrak{C} \models \Box\psi$ iff $\Box\psi \in \mathrm{ClTr}(\mathcal{KK})$*

- *If $\mathfrak{C} \models \mathrm{ClTr}(\mathcal{KK})$, then $\mathfrak{C} \models \blacksquare\psi$ iff $\blacksquare\psi \in \mathrm{ClTr}(\mathcal{KK})$*

- *If $\mathrm{ClTr}(\mathcal{KK}) \models \{\Diamond\psi, \blacklozenge\psi\}$ and $\mathcal{KK}$ is satisfiable, then $\psi \notin \mathcal{T}_{\mathcal{KK}} \cup \mathcal{F}_{\mathcal{KK}}$.*

- *At least one of the formulae $\Box\psi$, $\blacksquare\psi$, $\Diamond\psi$ or $\blacklozenge\psi$ is an element of $\mathrm{ClTr}(\mathcal{KK})$.*

- $\mathrm{Cont}(\psi, \mathrm{eval}_{\mathcal{KK}}(\psi)) \subseteq \mathrm{ClTr}(\mathcal{KK})$.

- *Let*

$$\mathcal{VK} := (\{\eta \in \mathcal{L} \mid \Box\eta \in \mathrm{ClTr}(\mathcal{KK})\}, \{\eta \in \mathcal{L} \mid \blacksquare\eta \in \mathrm{ClTr}(\mathcal{KK})\})$$

then $\mathrm{eval}_{\mathcal{KK}}(\psi) = \mathrm{eval}_{\mathcal{VK}}(\psi)$ and

$$\mathcal{VK} = \left(\{\psi \in \mathcal{L} \mid \mathcal{KK} \models \psi\}, \{\psi \in \mathcal{L} \mid \mathcal{KK} \overset{co}{\models} \psi\} \right). \qquad \Box$$

Lemma 5.1.5 (Cloud-Translation Preserves Satisfiability)

Let $\mathcal{KK}$ be a knowledge-base. Then $\mathcal{KK}$ is satisfiable iff $\mathrm{ClTr}(\mathcal{KK})$ is satisfiable. □

PROOF Left to right:

Let $U := \{ \psi \in \mathcal{L} \mid u = \mathrm{eval}_{\mathcal{KK}}(\psi) \}$.

Assume $U \neq \emptyset$.

By definition of the evaluation for all $\psi \in U$ there are interpretations i_ψ and j_ψ,

such that $i_\psi \vDash (\mathcal{T}_{\mathcal{KK}} \cup \{\psi\}, \mathcal{F}_{\mathcal{KK}})$ and $j_\psi \vDash (\mathcal{T}_{\mathcal{KK}}, \mathcal{F}_{\mathcal{KK}} \cup \{\psi\})$.

Define $\mathfrak{C}$ by $W_{\mathfrak{C}} := U \times \{t, f\}$ and $\iota_{\mathfrak{C}}$ by setting $\iota_{\mathfrak{C}}((\psi, t)) := i_\psi$ and $\iota_{\mathfrak{C}}((\psi, f)) := j_\psi$. Hence by choice of i_ψ and j_ψ the following are immediate:

- $\mathfrak{C} \vDash \Box\varphi$ for all φ with $\mathrm{eval}_{\mathcal{KK}}(\varphi) = t$,

- $\mathfrak{C} \vDash \blacksquare\varphi$ for all φ with $\mathrm{eval}_{\mathcal{KK}}(\varphi) = f$,

- $\mathfrak{C} \vDash \Diamond\psi$ for all ψ with $\mathrm{eval}_{\mathcal{KK}}(\psi) = u$ ($\psi \in U$) and

- $\mathfrak{C} \vDash \blacklozenge\psi$ for all ψ with $\mathrm{eval}_{\mathcal{KK}}(\psi) = u$ ($\psi \in U$).

Therefore $\mathfrak{C} \vDash \mathrm{ClTr}(\mathcal{KK})$.

If $U = \emptyset$ (meaning $\mathcal{KK}$ is complete), assume $\mathfrak{k} \vDash \mathcal{KK}$.

Then we have that $\mathfrak{C}$ with $W_{\mathfrak{C}} = \{w\}$ and $\iota_{\mathfrak{C}}(w) := \mathfrak{k}$ is a model of $\mathrm{ClTr}(\mathcal{KK})$ as is easily seen.

Right to left:

Let $\mathfrak{C}$ be a model of $\mathrm{ClTr}(\mathcal{K}\!\mathcal{C})$. By definition

$$\mathfrak{C} \vDash \{\Box\psi \mid t = \mathsf{eval}_{\mathcal{K}\!\mathcal{C}}(\psi)\} \cup \{\blacksquare\psi \mid f = \mathsf{eval}_{\mathcal{K}\!\mathcal{C}}(\psi)\}.$$

Hence for any $w \in W_{\mathfrak{C}}$ it is $\iota_{\mathfrak{C}}(w) \vDash \mathcal{K}\!\mathcal{C}$. ∎

Lemma 5.1.6 (Truth by Cloud-Translation)

A censor censor *is truthful iff for every privacy configuration* $\mathcal{PC} = (\mathcal{CK}, \mathcal{AK}, \mathcal{SK})$, *every query sequence* $\mathbf{q}$ *and every* $n \in \mathbb{N}_0$ *we have*

$$\mathrm{ClTr}(\mathcal{CK}) \vDash \mathscr{H}_{\mathcal{PC},\mathbf{q}}(n).$$ □

PROOF Left to right:

We show $\mathscr{H}_{\mathcal{PC},\mathbf{q}}(n) \subseteq \mathrm{ClTr}(\mathcal{CK})$ by induction on n:

Since $\mathcal{CK} \vDash \mathcal{AK}$, then, for every $\psi \in \mathcal{T}_{\mathcal{AK}}$, we have that $\mathsf{eval}_{\mathcal{CK}}(\psi) = t$. Likewise, we have for every $\psi \in \mathcal{F}_{\mathcal{AK}}$, that $\mathsf{eval}_{\mathcal{CK}}(\psi) = f$

Hence

$$\mathscr{H}_{\mathcal{PC},\mathbf{q}}(0) = \{\Box\psi \mid \psi \in \mathcal{T}_{\mathcal{AK}}\} \cup \{\blacksquare\psi \mid \psi \in \mathcal{T}_{\mathcal{AK}}\}$$
$$= \bigcup_{\psi \in \mathcal{AK}} \mathrm{Cont}(\psi, \mathsf{eval}_{\mathcal{CK}}(\psi)) \subseteq \mathrm{ClTr}(\mathcal{CK})$$

Step: Since censor$_{\mathcal{PC}}$ is truthful, $a_{n+1} \in \{r, \mathsf{eval}_{\mathcal{CK}}(q_{n+1})\}$. Thus either

$$\mathscr{H}_{\mathcal{PC},\mathbf{q}}(n+1) = \mathscr{H}_{\mathcal{PC},\mathbf{q}}(n) \cup \mathrm{Cont}(q_{n+1}, r) = \mathscr{H}_{\mathcal{PC},\mathbf{q}}(n)$$

and we are done by I.H. or

$$\mathscr{H}_{\mathcal{PC},\mathbf{q}}(n+1) = \mathscr{H}_{\mathcal{PC},\mathbf{q}}(n) \cup \mathrm{Cont}(q_{n+1}, \mathsf{eval}_{\mathcal{CK}}(q_{n+1}))$$

which follows by I.H. and $\text{Cont}(q_{n+1}, \text{eval}_{\mathcal{C\!K}}(q_{n+1})) \subseteq \text{ClTr}(\mathcal{C\!K})$ by definition of ClTr.

Right to left:
Assume there is an index n, s.t. $a_n \notin \{r, \text{eval}_{\mathcal{C\!K}}(q_n)\}$. Wlog. let this index be minimal for $\mathbf{q}$. Let $\mathfrak{C}$ be a cloud model, s.t. $\mathfrak{C} \vDash \mathscr{H}_{\mathcal{R\!C}, \mathbf{q}}(n)$. Then $\mathfrak{C} \nvDash \text{Cont}(q_n, \text{eval}(\mathcal{C\!K}, q_n))$ by Lemma 5.1.1. Hence (in fact) no model $\mathfrak{C}$ of $\mathscr{H}_{\mathcal{R\!C}, \mathbf{q}}(n)$ satisfies $\mathfrak{C} \vDash \text{ClTr}(\mathcal{C\!K})$. But By Lemma 5.1.5 there is at least one model of $\text{ClTr}(\mathcal{C\!K})$, since $\mathcal{C\!K}$ is satisfiable by definition of privacy configuration. We conclude that this model of $\text{ClTr}(\mathcal{C\!K})$ cannot be a model of $\mathscr{H}_{\mathcal{R\!C}, \mathbf{q}}(n)$ and, therefore, $\text{ClTr}(\mathcal{C\!K}) \nvDash \mathscr{H}_{\mathcal{R\!C}, \mathbf{q}}(n)$ as required. ∎

The previous two lemmata combine very nicely:

Corollary 5.1.7
Every truthful censor is credible. □

5.1.2 Ignorance

In this section we show that a given answer u does not have any implicational strength when considering general knowledge-bases. As we show in section 5.3 this turns out to be a valuable tool when dealing with lying censors: answers that would violate privacy can simply be replaced by u in order to maintain privacy. However, even when dealing with truthful censors it is quite helpful since it also removes the need to check for a possible privacy violation in the cases where the query directly evaluates to u.

Lemma 5.1.8

Let $\varphi, \eta \in \mathcal{L}$ and let $\mathsf{censor}_{\mathcal{R}}$ be a censor. Further assume that each of $\Diamond\varphi$, $\blacklozenge\varphi$, and $\Diamond\eta$ is consistent with $\mathscr{H}_{\mathcal{R},\mathbf{q}}(n)$. Then if

$$\mathscr{H}_{\mathcal{R},\mathbf{q}}(n) \cup \mathrm{Cont}(\varphi, u) \vDash \Box\eta.$$

it follows $\mathscr{H}_{\mathcal{R},\mathbf{q}}(n) \vDash \Box\eta$.

Likewise, if $\blacklozenge\eta$ is consistent with $\mathscr{H}_{\mathcal{R},\mathbf{q}}(n)$, then if

$$\mathscr{H}_{\mathcal{R},\mathbf{q}}(n) \cup \mathrm{Cont}(\varphi, u) \vDash \blacksquare\eta,$$

it follows $\mathscr{H}_{\mathcal{R},\mathbf{q}}(n) \vDash \blacksquare\eta$. □

PROOF Since $\Diamond\varphi, \blacklozenge\varphi$ are satisfiable in $\mathscr{H}_{\mathcal{R},\mathbf{q}}(n)$, there are cloud-models

$$\mathfrak{L} \vDash \mathscr{H}_{\mathcal{R},\mathbf{q}}(n) \cup \{\Diamond\varphi\} \quad \text{and} \quad \mathfrak{M} \vDash \mathscr{H}_{\mathcal{R},\mathbf{q}}(n) \cup \{\blacklozenge\varphi\}.$$

Hence there are worlds $l \in W_{\mathfrak{L}}$ and $m \in W_{\mathfrak{M}}$ with $\mathcal{I} := \iota_{\mathfrak{L}}(l) \vDash \varphi$, $\mathcal{J} := \iota_{\mathfrak{M}}(m) \overset{\mathrm{co}}{\vDash} \varphi$ and for all formulae $\rho \in \mathcal{L}$, s.t. $\Box\rho \in \mathscr{H}_{\mathcal{R},\mathbf{q}}(n)$, it holds $\mathcal{I} \vDash \rho$ and $\mathcal{J} \vDash \rho$.

Likewise for all formulae $\rho \in \mathcal{L}$, s.t. $\blacksquare\rho \in \mathscr{H}_{\mathcal{R},\mathbf{q}}(n)$, it holds $\mathcal{I} \overset{\mathrm{co}}{\vDash} \rho$ and $\mathcal{J} \overset{\mathrm{co}}{\vDash} \rho$.

Let $\mathfrak{C}$ be an arbitrary cloud-model of $\mathscr{H}_{\mathcal{R},\mathbf{q}}(n)$ and $w \in W_{\mathfrak{C}}$. Then in $\iota_{\mathfrak{C}}(w)$ it either φ is satisfied or co-satisfied. Assume φ is satisfied: By adding a fresh world j to $W_{\mathfrak{C}}$ with $\iota_{\mathfrak{C}}(j) = \mathcal{J}$ we obtain a new model that satisfies $\mathscr{H}_{\mathcal{R},\mathbf{q}}(n) \cup \mathrm{Cont}(\varphi, u)$, since by construction all $\Box$- and $\blacksquare$-formulae are satisfied and for each $\Diamond$-formula there is at least one world satisfying the corresponding $\mathcal{L}$-formula. Let us point out, that this is sufficient only because there are no logical connectives that combine cloud-formulae, especially no kind of disjunction or negation.

Thus by presumption this model satisfies $\Box \eta$. Therefore by definition η is satisfied in all $\iota(w)$ where $w \in W_{\mathfrak{C}} \cup \{j\}$. Hence η is satisfied in all $\iota(w)$ where $w \in W_{\mathfrak{C}}$ and hence $\mathfrak{C} \vDash \Box \eta$.

The case, in which φ is co-satisfied, follows analogously by adding $\mathcal{I}$.

The second part of the lemma follows similarly. ∎

Corollary 5.1.9 (Security in Ignorance)

Let censor *be a censor. For privacy configuration $\mathcal{PC}$, query-sequence $\mathbf{q} \in \mathcal{L}^{\mathbb{N}}$ and $\mathbf{a} := \text{censor}_{\mathcal{PC}, \mathcal{PC}}(\mathbf{q})$, let* censor$_{\mathcal{PC}}$ *fulfil the conditions* $\left(C^n_{\mathcal{PC}, \mathbf{q}}\right)$, $\left(E^n_{\mathcal{PC}, \mathbf{q}}\right)$, *and* $\left(\bar{E}^n_{\mathcal{PC}, \mathbf{q}}\right)$.

If both $\Diamond q_{n+1}$ and $\blacklozenge q_{n+1}$ are satisfiable in $\mathscr{H}_{\mathcal{PC}, \mathbf{q}}(n)$ then setting the corresponding answer to $a_{n+1} := u$ leads to satisfaction of the conditions $\left(C^{n+1}_{\mathcal{PC}, \mathbf{q}}\right)$, $\left(E^{n+1}_{\mathcal{PC}, \mathbf{q}}\right)$ and $\left(\overline{E}^{n+1}_{\mathcal{PC}, \mathbf{q}}\right)$. □

5.1.3 Standard Repudiation Sequences

Basically repudiation is a property that enforces the existence of alternative, non-harmful knowledge-bases. These knowledge-bases should act as replacement of the censored knowledge-base and the censor should reproduce the same answers when equipped with those alternatives. This way, meta-inference by reverse engineering possible databases and hence revealing hidden secrets by an attacker is effectively blocked.

A good candidate as such a cover-up-sequence of knowledge-bases turns out to be

$$\mathit{Alt}_{\mathcal{K}}(n) := (\{\psi \mid \Box\psi \in \mathscr{K}_{\mathcal{RC},\mathbf{q}}(n)\}, \{\psi \mid \blacksquare\psi \in \mathscr{K}_{\mathcal{RC},\mathbf{q}}(n)\})$$

at least for effective censors. The main reason is the following fact:

Proposition 5.1.10

For all $n \in \mathbb{N}$ and $\psi \in \mathcal{L}$, if a censor is effective up to stage n it holds

$$\mathscr{K}_{\mathcal{RC},\mathbf{q}}(n) \vDash \Box\psi \text{ iff } \mathit{Alt}_{\mathcal{K}}(n) \vDash \psi,$$

and

$$\mathscr{K}_{\mathcal{RC},\mathbf{q}}(n) \vDash \blacksquare\psi \text{ iff } \mathit{Alt}_{\mathcal{K}}(n) \overset{co}{\vDash} \psi. \qquad \Box$$

PROOF Concerning the first part:

Right to left is trivial.

By effectiveness it exists a model of $\mathscr{K}_{\mathcal{RC},\mathbf{q}}(n)$.

Assume $\mathit{Alt}_{\mathcal{K}}(n) \nvDash \psi$.

Let $\mathfrak{M} \vDash \mathscr{K}_{\mathcal{RC},\mathbf{q}}(n)$ and $\mathcal{I} \vDash \mathit{Alt}_{\mathcal{K}}(n)$ with $\mathcal{I} \nvDash \psi$.

Then the model constructed by $\mathfrak{N} = (W_{\mathfrak{N}}, \iota_{\mathfrak{N}})$ with $W_{\mathfrak{N}} := W_{\mathfrak{M}} \cup \{i\}$ and

$$\iota_{\mathfrak{N}}(w) = \begin{cases} \iota_{\mathfrak{M}}(w) & \text{if} \quad w \in W_{\mathfrak{M}} \\ \mathcal{I} & \text{if} \quad w = i \end{cases}$$

is a model of $\mathscr{K}_{\mathcal{RC},\mathbf{q}}(n)$. But $\mathfrak{N} \nvDash \Box\psi$.

Concerning the second part: Co-satisfaction is a stronger notion than satisfiability, since it requires an interpretation to exist.

So if $\mathit{Alt}_{\mathcal{K}} \overset{co}{\nvDash} \psi$, there are two cases: $\mathit{Alt}_{\mathcal{K}}$ is not satisfiable or it has an interpretation $\mathcal{I} \vDash \mathit{Alt}_{\mathcal{K}}(n)$, where $\mathcal{I} \vDash \psi$.

The first case can not happen, because since by effectiveness, there is a model $\mathfrak{M} \vDash \mathscr{H}_{\mathcal{PC},\mathbf{q}}(n)$. But for all worlds $w \in W_{\mathfrak{M}}$ of this model we have for all named interpretations: $\iota_{\mathfrak{C}}(w) \vDash \mathscr{Alt}_{\mathcal{C}}$.

Hence the second case applies, where the statement follows similar as the proof of the first part of the lemma. ∎

Corollary 5.1.11

Let censor *be truthful. Then* $\mathcal{C\!K} \vDash \mathscr{Alt}_{\mathcal{C}}(n)$ *for any privacy configuration* $\mathcal{PC}$ *and all* n. □

PROOF Let $\psi \in \mathcal{T}_{\mathscr{Alt}_{\mathcal{C}}(n)}$.

By proposition 5.1.10 $\mathscr{H}_{\mathcal{PC},\mathbf{q}}(n) \vDash \Box\psi$. Hence by lemma 5.1.6 it is $\mathrm{ClTr}(\mathcal{C\!K}) \vDash \Box\psi$. By definition of the cloud translation it follows $\Box\psi \in \mathrm{ClTr}(\mathcal{C\!K})$ and by the same definition $\mathcal{C\!K} \vDash \psi$.

Similarly follows $\mathcal{C\!K} \overset{co}{\vDash} \psi$, when $\psi \in \mathcal{F}_{\mathscr{Alt}_{\mathcal{C}}(n)}$.

5.2 Truthful Censors

In this section the censors must be truthful. So they might refuse to answer every query, meaning in this context assigning r as answer, but they cannot assign an answer from $\{t, f, u\}$ that differs from the actual evaluation.

An interesting point in this setting is the possibility to complete the separation of effectiveness from repudiation. To this end we will discuss two truthful censors which are both continuous, effective and credible, but only one is repudiating. The failure of being repudiating will also show how a leak of the censor algorithm can present a way of obtaining secrets.

Algorithm 1 Calculate $\mathsf{RTCens}_{\mathcal{PC}}(\mathbf{q})$

Require: $\mathcal{PC} = (\mathcal{CK}, \mathcal{SK}, \mathcal{AK})$ as privacy configuration
Require: $\mathbf{q} \in \mathcal{L}^{\mathbb{N}}$
 1: $\mathbf{a} = (a_1, a_2, \ldots) \leftarrow (u, u, \ldots)$
 2: $\mathscr{H}_{\mathcal{PC},\mathbf{q}}(0) \leftarrow \bigcup\limits_{\varphi \in \mathcal{T}_{\mathcal{AK}}} \mathrm{Cont}(\varphi, t) \cup \bigcup\limits_{\varphi \in \mathcal{F}_{\mathcal{AK}}} \mathrm{Cont}(\varphi, f)$
 3: **for** $n \leftarrow 1 \ldots \infty$ **do**
 4:     compliant $\leftarrow$ **true**
 5:     **for** $\sigma \in \mathcal{T}_{\mathcal{SK}}$ **do**
 6:        **if** $\mathscr{H}_{\mathcal{PC},\mathbf{q}}(n-1) \cup \mathrm{Cont}(q_n, t) \vDash \Box\sigma$
           or $\mathscr{H}_{\mathcal{PC},\mathbf{q}}(n-1) \cup \mathrm{Cont}(q_n, f) \vDash \Box\sigma$ **then**
 7:           $a_n \leftarrow r$
 8:           compliant $\leftarrow$ **false**
 9:        **end if**
10:     **end for**
11:     **for** $\sigma \in \mathcal{F}_{\mathcal{SK}}$ **do**
12:        **if** $\mathscr{H}_{\mathcal{PC},\mathbf{q}}(n-1) \cup \mathrm{Cont}(q_n, t) \vDash \blacksquare\sigma$
           or $\mathscr{H}_{\mathcal{PC},\mathbf{q}}(n-1) \cup \mathrm{Cont}(q_n, f) \vDash \blacksquare\sigma$ **then**
13:           $a_n \leftarrow r$
14:           compliant $\leftarrow$ **false**
15:        **end if**
16:     **end for**
17:     **if** compliant **then**
18:        $a_n \leftarrow \mathsf{eval}_{\mathcal{CK}}(q_n)$
19:     **end if**
20:     $\mathscr{H}_{\mathcal{PC},\mathbf{q}}(n) \leftarrow \mathscr{H}_{\mathcal{PC},\mathbf{q}}(n-1) \cup \mathrm{Cont}(q_n, a_n)$
21: **end for**
22: **return a**

Algorithm 2 Calculate $\mathsf{TCens}_{\mathcal{PC}}(\mathbf{q})$

Require: $\mathcal{PC} = (\mathcal{CK}, \mathcal{SK}, \mathcal{AK})$ as privacy configuration
Require: $\mathbf{q} \in \mathcal{L}^{\mathbb{N}}$

1: $\mathbf{a} = (a_1, a_2, \ldots) \leftarrow (u, u, \ldots)$

2: $\mathscr{H}_{\mathcal{PC},\mathbf{q}}(0) \quad \bigcup_{\varphi \in \mathcal{T}_{\mathcal{AK}}} \mathrm{Cont}(\varphi, t) \cup \bigcup_{\varphi \in \mathcal{F}_{\mathcal{AK}}} \mathrm{Cont}(\varphi, f)$

3: **for** $n \leftarrow 1 \ldots \infty$ **do**

4:     compliant $\leftarrow$ **true**

5:     $p \leftarrow \mathsf{eval}_{\mathcal{CK}}(q_n)$

6:     **for** $\sigma \in \mathcal{T}_{\mathcal{SK}}$ **do**

7:         **if** $\mathscr{H}_{\mathcal{PC},\mathbf{q}}(n-1) \cup \mathrm{Cont}(q_n, p) \vDash \square\sigma$ **then**

8:             $a_n \leftarrow r$

9:             compliant $\leftarrow$ **false**

10:         **end if**

11:     **end for**

12:     **for** $\sigma \in \mathcal{F}_{\mathcal{SK}}$ **do**

13:         **if** $\mathscr{H}_{\mathcal{PC},\mathbf{q}}(n-1) \cup \mathrm{Cont}(q_n, p) \vDash \blacksquare\sigma$ **then**

14:             $a_n \leftarrow r$

15:             compliant $\leftarrow$ **false**

16:         **end if**

17:     **end for**

18:     **if** compliant **then**

19:         $a_n \leftarrow p$

20:     **end if**

21:     $\mathscr{H}_{\mathcal{PC},\mathbf{q}}(n) \leftarrow \mathscr{H}_{\mathcal{PC},\mathbf{q}}(n-1) \cup \mathrm{Cont}(q_n, a_n)$

22: **end for**

23: **return** $\mathbf{a}$

Definition 5.2.1 (Truthful Censors)
We denote the censor determined by algorithm 1 as RTCens (repudiating, not minimally invasive truthful censor) and the censor determined by algorithm 2 as TCens (non repudiating, minimally invasive truthful censor). □

The difference between both algorithms is the choice when they refuse to answer. The censor TCens only refuses if a truthful answer leads to a $\mathcal{H}_{\mathcal{PC},\mathbf{q}}(\cdot)$ in which a secret is violated. The censor RTCens also refuses when a response of t or f would lead to this violation of effectiveness. It is immediately clear that RTCens is not minimally invasive.

At a first glance and having corollary 5.1.9 in mind it appears, that RTCens should also answer unknown, if that is the evaluated answer. However this would lead to a censor violating repudiation.

Example 5.2.2 (Non-Repudiation in Truthful Ignorance)
Assume RTCens would answer u, whenever $\text{eval}_{\mathcal{CK}}(q_i) = u$. In this case the proofs of continuity, truth, credibility and effectiveness given in the coming lemmata still work fine (after shifting around some cases). We give a counter example to show a failure in repudiation: Assume $\mathcal{PC} := (\mathcal{CK}, \mathcal{AK}, \mathcal{SK})$ with

- $\mathcal{CK} := (\emptyset, \{\sigma\})$,

- $\mathcal{AK} := (\emptyset, \emptyset)$ and

- $\mathcal{SK} := (\emptyset, \{\sigma, \rho\})$,

with $\sigma, \rho \in \mathbb{P}_{\{a,b,c,\dots\}}$.
We ask the query sequence

84

$$\mathbf{q} := (\sigma \wedge \rho, \rho, \sigma, a \wedge \neg a, a \wedge \neg a, \ldots).$$

As is easily calculated, we get:

$$\mathsf{eval}_{\mathcal{O}\!\mathcal{K}}(\sigma \wedge \rho) = f$$
$$\mathsf{eval}_{\mathcal{O}\!\mathcal{K}}(\rho) = u$$
$$\mathsf{eval}_{\mathcal{O}\!\mathcal{K}}(\sigma) = f$$

It is simple to infer the answer given by the modified $\mathsf{RTCens}_{\mathcal{RC}}$ (with unknown):

$$\mathbf{a} = (f, u, r, f, \ldots)$$

The violation of repudiation happens after the refusal:

First notice that after the second answer, any knowledge-base $(\mathcal{T}, \mathcal{F})$ that produces the same answers has to semantically co-imply $\sigma \wedge \rho$, but must also not imply or co-imply ρ. Hence there are two options left for σ: either it evaluates to u (meaning $\sigma \wedge \rho$ is a consequence of more complex axioms) or it evaluates to f. Since in the first case our modified censor would answer u, which it does not ($a_3 = r$), there is only one option left and this is $\mathsf{eval}_{(\mathcal{T},\mathcal{F})}(\sigma) = f$.   □

Example 5.2.3 (3.2.2 cont'd)

Let us calculate the answers of both truthful censors in the case where TheCar $\equiv P$:

$$\mathsf{TCens}\ldots(\mathbf{P}^1) = (f, f, f, f, r, r, t, t, \ldots)$$

$$\mathsf{TCens}\ldots(\mathbf{P}^2) = (t, t, t, t, t, r, r, t, t, \ldots)$$

The non-repudiating censor refuses to answer on two questions in both sequences. In $\mathbf{P}^1$, since correctly answering f to $\exists\mathsf{DriverOf}.P \equiv$

85

D, would already imply $\exists \mathrm{DriverOf}.P \equiv F$ to be true in any interpretation.

Similarly in the answer to $\mathbf{P}^2$.

However, in contrast to example 5.2.2 above, Floyd is still not lost when the policeman knows the algorithm, since it is clear, that f would be a safe answer to $\exists \mathrm{DriverOf}.P \equiv E$, as well as $\exists \mathrm{DriverOf}.P \equiv F$. So both cases remain as possible interpretations.

For the repudiating version, we obtain the answers:

$$\mathsf{RTCens}\ldots(\mathbf{P}^1) = (r, r, r, r, r, r, t, t, \ldots)$$

$$\mathsf{RTCens}\ldots(\mathbf{P}^2) = (t, t, t, t, t, r, r, t, t, \ldots)$$

In the first answer, since every answer to true would immediately yield a secret. And in the second query's answer, which is the same answer that TCens gave to $\mathbf{P}^2$, by understanding that changing any of the given r to either f or t would give away one of the community-members as driver. However, the given answer rules out A, B, C and D as possible drivers. $\qquad\square$

The continuity of both censors is immediate:

Lemma 5.2.4 (Continuity)

The censors RTCens *and* TCens *are continuous.* $\qquad\square$

PROOF Clear by inspection of the algorithm: All decisions are based only on the state-clouds that are constructed in a step before and the current query. $\qquad\blacksquare$

Lemma 5.2.5 (Truth)

The censors RTCens *and* TCens *are truthful.* $\qquad\square$

PROOF In both algorithms the answer is only modified to r (if at all). Hence the condition $a_n \in \{r, \text{eval}_{\mathcal{O}_C}(q_n)\}$ is always satisfied. ∎

The previous lemma in combination with corollary 5.1.7 provides immediately:

Corollary 5.2.6 (Credibility)
The censors RTCens *and* TCens *are credible.* □

Lemma 5.2.7 (Effectiveness)
The censors RTCens *and* TCens *are effective.* □

PROOF Let $\text{censor}_{\mathcal{PC}} \in \{\text{RTCens}, \text{TCens}\}$, $\mathcal{PC}$ be a privacy configuration and $\mathbf{q}$ be a query sequence. Set $\mathbf{a} := \text{censor}_{\mathcal{PC}\,\mathcal{PC}}(\mathbf{q})$ and assume that for all $m < n$ the required properties - for all $\sigma \in \mathcal{T}_{\mathcal{SC}}$ not $\mathscr{SC}_{\mathcal{PC},\mathbf{q}}(m) \vDash \Box \sigma$ and for all $\sigma \in \mathcal{F}_{\mathcal{SC}}$ not $\mathscr{SC}_{\mathcal{PC},\mathbf{q}}(m) \vDash \blacksquare \sigma$ - holds. We prove that for n this holds as well:

Case $\text{eval}_{\mathcal{O}_C}(q_n) = u$:

For both TCens and RTCens: In case u is selected as answer, effectiveness in stage n is immediate from corollary 5.1.9. Only RTCens can also refuse in this case. Then it is

$$\mathscr{SC}_{\mathcal{PC},\mathbf{q}}(n) = \mathscr{SC}_{\mathcal{PC},\mathbf{q}}(n-1) \cup \emptyset = \mathscr{SC}_{\mathcal{PC},\mathbf{q}}(n-1)$$

and the property follows by induction hypothesis.

Case $\text{eval}_{\mathcal{O}_C}(q_n) = t$ (for both censors):

If the property is violated, there is a $\sigma \in \mathcal{T}_{\mathcal{SC}}$, s.t. $\mathscr{SC}_{\mathcal{PC},\mathbf{q}}(n) \vDash \Box \sigma$ or a $\sigma \in \mathcal{F}_{\mathcal{SC}}$, s.t. $\mathscr{SC}_{\mathcal{PC},\mathbf{q}}(n) \vDash \blacksquare \sigma$. But, by construction of the state-cloud, we have

$$\mathscr{SC}_{\mathcal{PC},\mathbf{q}}(n) = \mathscr{SC}_{\mathcal{PC},\mathbf{q}}(n-1) \cup \text{Cont}(q_n, t)$$

and hence, in case $\sigma \in \mathcal{T}_{\mathcal{SK}}$, we have $\mathscr{H}_{\mathcal{RC},\mathbf{q}}(n-1) \cup \mathrm{Cont}(q_n, t) \vDash \Box\sigma$ in contradiction to the refusal-selection in line 7 in TCens and line 6 in RTCens, respectively. In the other case, $\sigma \in \mathcal{F}_{\mathcal{SK}}$, analougously we have $\mathscr{H}_{\mathcal{RC},\mathbf{q}}(n-1) \cup \mathrm{Cont}(q_n, t) \vDash \blacksquare\sigma$, in contradicting to the refusal-selection in the corresponding line 13 in TCens and line 12 in RTCens, respectively.

Hence both censors would have refused to answer then leaving

$$\mathscr{H}_{\mathcal{RC},\mathbf{q}}(n) = \mathscr{H}_{\mathcal{RC},\mathbf{q}}(n-1) \cup \emptyset$$

and thus fulfilling the property by I.H.

Case $\mathrm{eval}_{\mathcal{CK}}(q_n) = f$ (for both censors): follows analogously. ∎

Lemma 5.2.8 (Repudiation)

The censor RTCens is repudiating. □

PROOF Let $\mathcal{RC} = (\mathcal{CK}, \mathcal{AK}, \mathcal{SK})$ be a privacy configuration and $\mathbf{q}$ be a query sequence. Set $\mathbf{a} := \mathrm{RTCens}_{\mathcal{RC}}(\mathbf{q})$.

We show that $\mathit{Alt}_{\mathcal{K}}(n)$ is a possible choice.

Ad R-C)): $\mathcal{RC}_n := (\mathit{Alt}_{\mathcal{K}}(n), \mathcal{AK}, \mathcal{SK})$ is a privacy configuration:

-PC-A): $\mathit{Alt}_{\mathcal{K}}(n) \vDash \mathcal{AK}$.

Lines 2 and 20 of algorithm 1 reflect the definition of a state cloud as given in definition 2.4.13.

Since by this definition it is

$$\mathscr{H}_{\mathcal{RC},\mathbf{q}}(n) \supseteq \{\Box\psi \mid \psi \in \mathcal{T}_{\mathcal{AK}}\} \cup \{\blacksquare\psi \mid \psi \in \mathcal{F}_{\mathcal{AK}}\} = \mathscr{H}_{\mathcal{RC},\mathbf{q}}(0),$$

we have $\mathcal{T}_{\mathcal{AK}} \subseteq \mathcal{T}_{\mathit{Alt}_{\mathcal{K}}(n)}$ and $\mathcal{F}_{\mathcal{AK}} \subseteq \mathcal{F}_{\mathit{Alt}_{\mathcal{K}}(n)}$.

-PC-B): $\mathit{Alt}_{\mathcal{K}}(n)$ are satisfiable as a consequence of credibility.

-PC-C): is obvious, since $\mathcal{SK}$ and $\mathcal{AK}$ are unchanged.

Ad R-B): By effectiveness and proposition 5.1.10.

Ad R-A): Let $\mathbf{b} := \mathsf{RTCens}_{(\mathit{Alt}_{\mathcal{K}}(n), \mathcal{A}_{\mathcal{K}}, \mathcal{S}_{\mathcal{K}})}(\mathbf{q})$.

To show: For $1 \leq i \leq n$ it is $a_i = b_i$.

Observe that

$$\mathscr{H}_{\mathcal{R}, \mathbf{q}}(0) = \mathscr{H}_{\mathcal{R}_n, \mathbf{q}}(0) = \bigcup_{\psi \in \mathcal{T}_{\mathcal{A}_{\mathcal{K}}}} \mathrm{Cont}(\psi, t) \cup \bigcup_{\psi \in \mathcal{F}_{\mathcal{A}_{\mathcal{K}}}} \mathrm{Cont}(\psi, f)$$

holds. Assume we have checked that $a_k = b_k$ for all $k < i \leq n$. Hence for those k (and especially $k = i - 1$)

$$\mathscr{H}_{\mathcal{R}, \mathbf{q}}(k) = \mathscr{H}_{\mathcal{R}_n, \mathbf{q}}(k) \qquad (\star)$$

Case $a_i = t$:
If $\mathscr{H}_{\mathcal{R}, \mathbf{q}}(i - 1) \vDash q_i$, by $(\star)$ also $\mathscr{H}_{\mathcal{R}_n, \mathbf{q}}(i - 1) \vDash q_i$. Hence we have $b_i = t$.

Else by $(\star)$: $\mathscr{H}_{\mathcal{R}_n, \mathbf{q}}(i-1) \cup \mathrm{Cont}(q_i, t)$ and $\mathscr{H}_{\mathcal{R}_n, \mathbf{q}}(i-1) \cup \mathrm{Cont}(q_i, f)$ do not imply any secret (otherwise already $a_i = r$).

Therefore $b_i := \mathsf{eval}(\mathit{Alt}_{\mathcal{K}}(n), q_i)$ must hold. But $q_i \in \mathit{Alt}_{\mathcal{K}}(n)$, since $\Box q_i \in \mathscr{H}_{\mathcal{R}, \mathbf{q}}(n)$.

Hence, it is $\mathsf{eval}(\mathit{Alt}_{\mathcal{K}}(n), q_i) = t$ and thus $b_i = t$.

Case $a_i = f$: analogous.

Case $a_i = u$: By $(\star)$ follows:

- $\mathscr{H}_{\mathcal{R}_n, \mathbf{q}}(i - 1) \nvDash \Box q_i$ and

- $\mathscr{H}_{\mathcal{R}_n, \mathbf{q}}(i - 1) \nvDash \blacksquare q_i$.

Also by $(\star)$ we obtain

- $\mathscr{H}_{\mathcal{R}_n, \mathbf{q}}(i - 1) \cup \mathrm{Cont}(q_i, t) \nvDash \Box \sigma$ and

- $\mathscr{H}_{\mathcal{PC}_n,\mathbf{q}}(i-1) \cup \mathrm{Cont}(q_i, f) \not\models \square\sigma$

for any $\sigma \in \mathcal{T}_{\mathcal{SK}}$ and

- $\mathscr{H}_{\mathcal{PC}_n,\mathbf{q}}(i-1) \cup \mathrm{Cont}(q_i, t) \not\models \blacksquare\sigma$ and

- $\mathscr{H}_{\mathcal{PC}_n,\mathbf{q}}(i-1) \cup \mathrm{Cont}(q_i, f) \not\models \blacksquare\sigma$

for any $\sigma \in \mathcal{F}_{\mathcal{SK}}$. Hence, with $\mathcal{CK} \models \mathit{Altk}(n)$ (corollary 5.1.11), it follows

$$b_i = \mathsf{eval}(\mathit{Altk}(n), q_i) = u.$$

Case $a_i = r$: Hence a positive secret (from $\mathcal{T}_{\mathcal{SK}}$) or negative secret (from $\mathcal{F}_{\mathcal{SK}}$) must have been violated.
If it is a positive secret,

- either $\mathscr{H}_{\mathcal{PC},\mathbf{q}}(i-1) \cup \{\square q_i\} \models \square\sigma$

- or $\mathscr{H}_{\mathcal{PC},\mathbf{q}}(i-1) \cup \{\blacksquare q_i\} \models \square\sigma$

for a $\sigma \in \mathcal{T}_{\mathcal{SK}}$. Hence by $(\star)$

- either $\mathscr{H}_{\mathcal{PC}_n,\mathbf{q}}(i-1) \cup \{\square q_i\} \models \square\sigma$

- or $\mathscr{H}_{\mathcal{PC}_n,\mathbf{q}}(i-1) \cup \{\square\neg q_i\} \models \square\sigma.$

Hence $b_i = r$.
If a negative secret is violated, this follows analogously. ∎

Lemma 5.2.9 (Minimally invasive)
The censor TCens *is minimally invasive.* □

PROOF Let $\mathcal{PC}$ be a privacy-configuration, $\mathbf{q}$ a query-sequence and set $\mathbf{a} := \mathsf{TCens}_{\mathcal{PC}}(\mathbf{q})$.

90

Assume there is an index i, s.t. $a_i \neq \mathsf{eval}_{\mathcal{K\!C}}(q_i)$. By inspection of the algorithm, this can only be a consequence of lines 8 or 14 setting $a_i = r$. Hence either by line 7 there is a secret $\sigma \in \mathcal{T}_{\mathcal{S\!C}}$ such that

$$\mathscr{H}_{\mathcal{R\!C},\mathbf{q}}(i-1) \cup \mathrm{Cont}(q_i, \mathsf{eval}_{\mathcal{K\!C}}(q_i)) \vDash \Box\sigma,$$

or by line 13 there is a secret $\sigma \in \mathcal{F}_{\mathcal{S\!C}}$ such that

$$\mathscr{H}_{\mathcal{R\!C},\mathbf{q}}(i-1) \cup \mathrm{Cont}(q_i, \mathsf{eval}_{\mathcal{K\!C}}(q_i)) \vDash \blacksquare\sigma,$$

in violation of effectiveness. ∎

Unfortunately, truthful censors have the problem, that either they have to be more uncooperative than one could hope for, or they are vulnerable to repudiation attacks that infer knowledge of secrets even if the state cloud does not semantically imply them. Hence, it is generally impossible for truthful censors to have all presented quality properties.

Theorem 5.2.10

A continuous truthful censor satisfies at most two of the properties effectiveness, minimal invasion and repudiation. □

PROOF Assume $\mathsf{censor}_{\mathcal{R\!C}}$ is continuous, truthful, credible, effective and minimally invasive. We will show that it is not repudiating. As above, examine the privacy-configuration $\mathcal{P\!C}$, given by

$$\mathcal{C\!C} := (\{\sigma\}, \emptyset), \quad \mathcal{A\!C} := (\emptyset, \emptyset) \quad \text{and} \quad \mathcal{S\!C} := (\{\sigma\}, \emptyset),$$

and the query $\mathbf{q} := (\sigma, \sigma, \dots)$. We set $\mathbf{a} := \mathsf{censor}_{\mathcal{R\!C}}(\mathbf{q})$. Obviously $a_1 = r$ must hold, otherwise $\mathsf{censor}_{\mathcal{R\!C}}$ either lies or reveals a se-

cret. Assume a censored knowledge-base $\mathcal{RK}_1$ as alternative to $\mathcal{CK}$ at stage 1 and define $\mathbf{a}' := \mathsf{censor}_{\mathcal{PC}\,\mathcal{RK}_1, \mathcal{AC}, \mathcal{SK}}(\mathbf{q})$.
There are three cases:

- $\mathcal{RK}_1 \vDash \sigma$

- $\mathcal{RK}_1 \overset{co}{\vDash} \sigma$

- both $\mathcal{RK}_1 \nvDash \sigma$ and $\mathcal{RK}_1 \overset{cp}{\nvDash} \sigma$

It suffices to show, that the later two cannot occur.
Assume $\mathcal{RK}_1 \overset{co}{\vDash} \sigma$.
As consequence of being truthful, the first answer must be either $a'_1 = f$ or $a'_1 = r$. By the fact $\mathcal{HC}_{\mathcal{PC},\mathbf{q}}(0) \cup \{\blacksquare\sigma\} \nvDash \Box\sigma$ and minimal invasion (it is the first given answer!) it follows that $a'_1 = f$ and hence we obtain the contradiction to $f = a'_1 \overset{!}{=} a_1 = r$.
Analogously in the third case it follows $a'_1 = u$.
Hence only knowledge-bases that semantically imply σ are possible alternatives to $\mathcal{CK}$, contradicting repudiation. ∎

Corollary 5.2.11 (Non-repudiation)
The censor TCens *is not repudiating.* □

Corollary 5.2.12
Effectiveness, continuity, credibility and minimal invasion do not imply repudiation. □

5.3 Cooperative Lying Censors

Since the refusing approach did turn out to be unsatisfying, we next want to consider a censor that is capable of lying but not refusing to answer.

Formally this means that they are not truthful, but the possible answers are limited to $\mathbb{A} = \{t, f, u\}$. Let us point out that one could adapt all proofs to the full answer set (including r) and require that a censor in any situation has an answer different from r. Such a censor is denoted (seemingly) *cooperative* (compare definition 2.4.22).

In this section we will discuss censors that are minimally invasive, lying and not refusing.

Definition 5.3.1 (Minimally Invasive Lying Censor)
We denote the censor determined by algorithm 3 as MILCens. □

Let us remark that the only difference to TCens is the replacement of the refusal in lines 8 and 14 with the answer u.

Example 5.3.2 (3.2.2 cont'd)
Calculating the answers of MILCens in the case where TheCar $\equiv P$ yields:

$$\text{MILCens}\ldots(\mathbf{P}^1) = (f, f, f, f, u, u, t, t, \ldots)$$

$$\text{MILCens}\ldots(\mathbf{P}^2) = (t, t, t, t, t, u, u, t, t, \ldots)$$

We find that the censor lies to answer on two questions in both sequences. Unsurprisingly the answers refused by TCens are now set to u for the same reasons TCens refused them. □

Lemma 5.3.3 (Continuity)
The censor MILCens *is continuous.* □

PROOF Clear by inspection of the algorithm: simply notice that the determination of the answer a_n in lines 8, 14 and 19 only depends on $\mathcal{H}_{\mathcal{R},\mathbf{q}}(n-1)$, which is determined in the prior loop, and the current query q_n. ■

Algorithm 3 Calculate $\mathsf{MILCens}_{\mathcal{PC}}(\mathbf{q})$

Require: $\mathcal{PC} = (\mathcal{CK}, \mathcal{SK}, \mathcal{AK})$ as privacy configuration
Require: $\mathbf{q} \in \mathcal{L}^{\mathbb{N}}$
1: $\mathbf{a} = (a_1, a_2, \ldots) \leftarrow (u, u, \ldots)$
2: $\mathscr{H}_{\mathcal{PC},\mathbf{q}}(0) \leftarrow \bigcup\limits_{\varphi \in \mathcal{T}_{\mathcal{AK}}} \mathrm{Cont}(\varphi, t) \cup \bigcup\limits_{\varphi \in \mathcal{F}_{\mathcal{AK}}} \mathrm{Cont}(\varphi, f)$
3: **for** $n \leftarrow 1 \ldots \infty$ **do**
4:      compliant $\leftarrow$ **true**
5:      $p \leftarrow \mathsf{eval}_{\mathcal{CK}}(q_n)$
6:      **for** $\sigma \in \mathcal{T}_{\mathcal{SK}}$ **do**
7:          **if** $\mathscr{H}_{\mathcal{PC},\mathbf{q}}(n-1) \cup \mathrm{Cont}(q_n, p) \vDash \Box\sigma$ **then**
8:              $a_n \leftarrow u$
9:              compliant $\leftarrow$ **false**
10:          **end if**
11:      **end for**
12:      **for** $\sigma \in \mathcal{F}_{\mathcal{SK}}$ **do**
13:          **if** $\mathscr{H}_{\mathcal{PC},\mathbf{q}}(n-1) \cup \mathrm{Cont}(q_n, p) \vDash \blacksquare\sigma$ **then**
14:              $a_n \leftarrow u$
15:              compliant $\leftarrow$ **false**
16:          **end if**
17:      **end for**
18:      **if** compliant **then**
19:          $a_n \leftarrow p$
20:      **end if**
21:      $\mathscr{H}_{\mathcal{PC},\mathbf{q}}(n) \leftarrow \mathscr{H}_{\mathcal{PC},\mathbf{q}}(n-1) \cup \mathrm{Cont}(q_n, a_n)$
22: **end for**
23: **return** $\mathbf{a}$

Proposition 5.3.4

For the state-clouds of the censor MILCens *holds: For all security configurations, query sequences and all* $n \in \mathbb{N}_0$:

$$\text{if } \Box\psi \in \mathscr{H}_{\mathcal{R},\mathbf{q}}(n), \text{ then } \text{eval}_{\mathcal{O}_{\mathcal{K}}}(\psi) = t,$$
$$\text{if } \blacksquare\psi \in \mathscr{H}_{\mathcal{R},\mathbf{q}}(n), \text{ then } \text{eval}_{\mathcal{O}_{\mathcal{K}}}(\psi) = f.$$

Furthermore $\mathcal{O}_{\mathcal{K}} \vDash \mathcal{A}lt_{\mathcal{K}}(n)$. □

PROOF By construction in the algorithm, if $\Box\psi \in \mathscr{H}_{\mathcal{R},\mathbf{q}}(n)$ [or resp. $\blacksquare\psi \in \mathscr{H}_{\mathcal{R},\mathbf{q}}(n)$] it results from line 2 or from line 5 in combination with line 19. In either case, by the definition of Cont, $\text{eval}_{\mathcal{O}_{\mathcal{K}}}(\psi) = t$ [$\text{eval}_{\mathcal{O}_{\mathcal{K}}}(\psi) = f$] is immediate. ∎

If $n = 0$ in the above proposition, then $\mathscr{H}_{\mathcal{R},\mathbf{q}}(n)$ encodes exactly the attacker's knowledge and hence the claim trivially holds by the conditions on privacy configurations.

Lemma 5.3.5 (Credibility, effectiveness)

The censor MILCens *is credible and effective.* □

PROOF Let $\mathbf{q}$ be a query-sequence, $\mathbf{a} := \text{censor}_{\mathcal{R}}(\mathbf{q})$ its answer-sequence and $n \in \mathbb{N}$. Assume that for all $m < n$ the required properties

$(C_{\mathcal{R},\mathbf{q}}^{m})$ $\mathscr{H}_{\mathcal{R},\mathbf{q}}(m)$ is satisfiable

$(E_{\mathcal{R},\mathbf{q}}^{m})$ for all $\sigma \in \mathcal{T}_{\mathcal{K}}$ not $\mathscr{H}_{\mathcal{R},\mathbf{q}}(m) \vDash \sigma$

$(\bar{E}_{\mathcal{R},\mathbf{q}}^{m})$ for all $\sigma \in \mathcal{F}_{\mathcal{K}}$ not $\mathscr{H}_{\mathcal{R},\mathbf{q}}(m) \overset{\text{co}}{\vDash} \sigma$

hold. We prove that for n these properties hold as well:
In case $\mathcal{K} = \emptyset$, this is immediate, since the censor will only give

true answers and $\mathcal{O}_{\!\mathcal{K}}$ is satisfiable.

Otherwise there are three cases:

First case: Assume $\mathrm{eval}_{\mathcal{O}_{\!\mathcal{K}}}(q_n) = t$:

There are four sub-cases:

(1) $\mathscr{H}_{\mathcal{R},\mathbf{q}}(n-1) \models \square q_n$: In this case $(C^n_{\mathcal{R},\mathbf{q}})$, $(E^n_{\mathcal{R},\mathbf{q}})$ and $(\bar{E}^n_{\mathcal{R},\mathbf{q}})$ are immediate.

(2) $\mathscr{H}_{\mathcal{R},\mathbf{q}}(n-1) \not\models \square q_n$ and no secret is violated by the next state-cloud, i.e. $\mathscr{H}_{\mathcal{R},\mathbf{q}}(n-1) \cup \mathrm{Cont}(q_n,t) \not\models \square\sigma$ for all $\sigma \in \mathcal{T}_{\mathcal{S}\!\mathcal{K}}$ and $\mathscr{H}_{\mathcal{R},\mathbf{q}}(n-1) \cup \mathrm{Cont}(q_n,t) \not\models \blacksquare\sigma$ for all $\sigma \in \mathcal{F}_{\mathcal{S}\!\mathcal{K}}$: Then $a_n = t$ is given by the algorithm and

$$\mathscr{H}_{\mathcal{R},\mathbf{q}}(n) = \mathscr{H}_{\mathcal{R},\mathbf{q}}(n-1) \cup \mathrm{Cont}(q_n,t)$$

is satisfiable, since otherwise in all models (there are none!) all secrets would be violated. Hence $(C^n_{\mathcal{R},\mathbf{q}})$, $(E^n_{\mathcal{R},\mathbf{q}})$ and $(\bar{E}^n_{\mathcal{R},\mathbf{q}})$ follow.

(3) $\mathscr{H}_{\mathcal{R},\mathbf{q}}(n-1) \not\models \square q_n$ and a secret is violated by the next state-cloud, i.e. $\mathscr{H}_{\mathcal{R},\mathbf{q}}(n-1) \cup \mathrm{Cont}(q_n,t) \models \square\sigma$ for a $\sigma \in \mathcal{T}_{\mathcal{S}\!\mathcal{K}}$ or $\mathscr{H}_{\mathcal{R},\mathbf{q}}(n-1) \cup \mathrm{Cont}(q_n,t) \models \blacksquare\sigma$ for a $\sigma \in \mathcal{F}_{\mathcal{S}\!\mathcal{K}}$: Then $a_n = u$ is returned. If $\mathscr{H}_{\mathcal{R},\mathbf{q}}(n) = \mathscr{H}_{\mathcal{R},\mathbf{q}}(n-1) \cup \mathrm{Cont}(q_n,u)$ would not be satisfiable, then either $\square q_n$ or $\blacksquare q_n$ is semantically implied by $\mathscr{H}_{\mathcal{R},\mathbf{q}}(n-1)$. The first being refused by assumption. If $\blacksquare q_n$ is semantically implied by $\mathscr{H}_{\mathcal{R},\mathbf{q}}(n-1)$, then by proposition 5.1.10 $\mathcal{A}l\!t_{\mathcal{K}}(n-1) \overset{\mathrm{co}}{\models} q_n$ and hence by proposition 5.3.4 $\mathcal{O}_{\!\mathcal{K}} \overset{\mathrm{co}}{\models} q_n$ contradicting $\mathrm{eval}_{\mathcal{O}_{\!\mathcal{K}}}(q_n) = t$. Hence we have $(C^m_{\mathcal{R},\mathbf{q}})$ and by lemma 5.1.9 follow $(E^n_{\mathcal{R},\mathbf{q}})$ and $(\bar{E}^n_{\mathcal{R},\mathbf{q}})$.

The case $\text{eval}_{\mathcal{O\!C}}(q_n) = f$ follows analogous.
The last case $\text{eval}_{\mathcal{O\!C}}(q_n) = u$: Obviously $a_n = u$ is returned. Satisfaction of the conditions $(C_{\mathcal{R\!C},\mathbf{q}}^n)$, $(E_{\mathcal{R\!C},\mathbf{q}}^n)$ and $(\bar{E}_{\mathcal{R\!C},\mathbf{q}}^n)$ follows as in sub-case (3) above. ∎

Lemma 5.3.6 (Minimally invasive and lying)
The censor MILCens is minimally invasive and lying. □

PROOF Ad "minimally invasive":
Assume $\mathbf{a} = \text{MILCens}_{\mathcal{R\!C}}(\mathbf{q})$ and $a_n \neq \text{eval}_{\mathcal{O\!C}}(q_n)$. Then a_n was set in line 8 or 14. By the corresponding security check in line 7 or 13 effectiveness would have been violated else.

Ad "lying":
We give a privacy configuration, a sequence of questions and an index such that the censor will lie:

$$\mathcal{O\!C} := (\{\sigma\}, \emptyset), \ \mathcal{A\!C} := (\emptyset, \emptyset), \ \mathcal{S\!C} := (\{\sigma\}, \emptyset) \text{ and } \mathbf{q} = (\sigma, \sigma, \ldots)$$

will produce $\mathbf{a} := (u, u, \ldots)$, but $a_1 = u \notin \{r, t = \text{eval}_{\mathcal{O\!C}}(q_1)\}$. ∎

Lemma 5.3.7 (Repudiation)
The censor MILCens is repudiating. □

PROOF Let $\mathbf{q}$ be a fixed question series and $\mathbf{a} = \text{MILCens}(\mathbf{q})$.
We show, that $\mathcal{A\!l\!t\!C}(n)$ is a possible choice of alternate databases:
From lemma 5.3.5 (effectiveness) and since

$$\{\Box\varphi \mid \varphi \in \mathcal{T}_{\mathcal{A\!l\!t\!C}(n)}\} \cup \{\blacksquare\varphi \mid \varphi \in \mathcal{F}_{\mathcal{A\!l\!t\!C}(n)}\} \subseteq \mathcal{S\!C}_{\mathcal{R\!C},\mathbf{q}}(n)$$

it follows that no secret is valid in $\mathcal{A\!l\!t\!C}(n)$, hence property R-B).

97

Ad R-A)): observe that each query q_i, where $i \leq n$, exactly one of the following holds:

- $q_i \in \mathcal{T}_{Alt_{\mathcal{K}}(n)}$ iff $Alt_{\mathcal{K}}(n) \vDash q_i$ iff $a_i = t$

- $q_i \in \mathcal{F}_{Alt_{\mathcal{K}}(n)}$ iff $Alt_{\mathcal{K}}(n) \overset{co}{\vDash} q_i$ iff $a_i = f$

- $q_i \notin \mathcal{T}_{Alt_{\mathcal{K}}(n)} \cup \mathcal{F}_{Alt_{\mathcal{K}}(n)}$ iff $Alt_{\mathcal{K}}(n) \nvDash q_i$ and $Alt_{\mathcal{K}}(n) \overset{co}{\nvDash} q_i$ iff $a_i = u$

This is immediate by credibility and construction.

Hence for all $i \leq n$ $\mathsf{eval}(Alt_{\mathcal{K}}(n), q_i) = a_i$.

Furthermore the security conditions from lines 7 and 13 of the algorithm are never satisfied, since otherwise by proposition 5.1.10 $Alt_{\mathcal{K}}(n)$ would violate this condition opposing lemma 5.3.5 (as above). Therefore all questions q_i, $i \leq n$, are answered by a_i and hence property R-A) follows.

Ad R-C)): Since satisfiability of $Alt_{\mathcal{K}}(n)$ was shown (PC-B)) and neither $A_{\mathcal{K}}$ nor $S_{\mathcal{K}}$ were changed (PC-C)), it remains to show that $Alt_{\mathcal{K}}(n) \vDash A_{\mathcal{K}}$ (PC-A)). This is immediate, since

$$\mathscr{H}_{\mathcal{PC},\mathbf{q}}(n) \supseteq \{\Box\psi \mid \psi \in \mathcal{T}_{A_{\mathcal{K}}}\} \cup \{\blacksquare\psi \mid \psi \in \mathcal{F}_{A_{\mathcal{K}}}\}$$

by construction. Therefore $A_{\mathcal{K}} \subseteq Alt_{\mathcal{K}}(n)$ and hence the proof. ∎

Example 5.3.8

Despite the last lemma, the censor is not atomic repudiating. Here we consider propositional logic over $\mathtt{A} := \{a, b, c, \ldots\}$.

Let $\mathcal{PC} = (C_{\mathcal{K}}, A_{\mathcal{K}}, S_{\mathcal{K}})$ be given by

- $C_{\mathcal{K}} := (\emptyset, \{a\})$

98

- $\mathcal{A}_{\mathcal{K}} := (\emptyset, \{a \wedge b\})$

- $\mathcal{S}_{\mathcal{K}} := (\emptyset, \{a\})$

Consider the query-sequence $\mathbf{q} = (b, b, \ldots)$ The censor MILCens would give the following answers

$$\text{MILCens}_{\mathcal{R}}(\mathbf{q} = (u, u, \ldots)$$

There are only two options that an atomic knowledge-base could cause the censor to answer u: The value is actually u, which implies, that the value of a is known to be f—violating a secret—, or b's value is t, which implies exactly the same. □

To finish the section, we give a non-effective (and thus also not minimally invasive) but credible censor, that satisfies repudiation. This will prove that repudiation does not imply effectiveness.

Definition 5.3.9 (Ineffective repudiating censor)
We denote the censor determined by algorithm 4 as IeRLCens. □

Lemma 5.3.10
The censor IeRLCens is credible. □

PROOF Observe that only the last else-clause in line 16 in the algorithm can lead to a not satisfiable $\mathscr{H}_{\mathcal{R},\mathbf{q}}(n)$ in line 19: when the algorithm answers within the first two checks the class of models of $\mathscr{H}_{\mathcal{R},\mathbf{q}}(n-1)$ and $\mathscr{H}_{\mathcal{R},\mathbf{q}}(n)$ remains the same. In the next four checks the desired satisfiability of the resulting $\mathscr{H}_{\mathcal{R},\mathbf{q}}(n)$ is an explicit condition.

Algorithm 4 Calculate $\mathsf{leRLCens}_{\mathcal{PC}}(\mathbf{q})$

Require: $\mathcal{PC} = (\mathcal{CK}, \mathcal{SK}, \mathcal{AK})$ as privacy configuration
Require: $\mathbf{q} \in \mathcal{L}^{\mathbb{N}}$
 1: $\mathbf{a} = (a_1, a_2, \ldots) \leftarrow (u, u, \ldots)$
 2: $\mathscr{SC}_{\mathcal{PC},\mathbf{q}}(0) \leftarrow \bigcup_{\varphi \in \mathcal{T_{AK}}} \mathrm{Cont}(\varphi, t) \cup \bigcup_{\varphi \in \mathcal{F_{AK}}} \mathrm{Cont}(\varphi, f)$
 3: **for** $n \leftarrow 1 \ldots \infty$ **do**
 4:   **if** $\mathscr{SC}_{\mathcal{PC},\mathbf{q}}(n-1) \vDash \mathrm{Cont}(q_n, t)$ **then**
 5:     $a_n \leftarrow t$
 6:   **else if** $\mathscr{SC}_{\mathcal{PC},\mathbf{q}}(n-1) \vDash \mathrm{Cont}(q_n, f)$ **then**
 7:     $a_n \leftarrow f$
 8:   **else if** $\mathscr{SC}_{\mathcal{PC},\mathbf{q}}(n-1) \cup \mathrm{Cont}(q_n, t)$ is satisfiable
       and $\mathscr{SC}_{\mathcal{PC},\mathbf{q}}(n-1) \cup \mathrm{Cont}(q_n, t) \vDash \Box\sigma$ for a $\sigma \in \mathcal{T_{SK}}$ **then**
 9:     $a_n \leftarrow t$
10:   **else if** $\mathscr{SC}_{\mathcal{PC},\mathbf{q}}(n-1) \cup \mathrm{Cont}(q_n, f)$ is satisfiable
       and $\mathscr{SC}_{\mathcal{PC},\mathbf{q}}(n-1) \cup \mathrm{Cont}(q_n, f) \vDash \Box\sigma$ for a $\sigma \in \mathcal{T_{SK}}$ **then**
11:     $a_n \leftarrow f$
12:   **else if** $\mathscr{SC}_{\mathcal{PC},\mathbf{q}}(n-1) \cup \mathrm{Cont}(q_n, t)$ is satisfiable
       and $\mathscr{SC}_{\mathcal{PC},\mathbf{q}}(n-1) \cup \mathrm{Cont}(q_n, t) \vDash \blacksquare\sigma$ for a $\sigma \in \mathcal{F_{SK}}$ **then**
13:     $a_n \leftarrow t$
14:   **else if** $\mathscr{SC}_{\mathcal{PC},\mathbf{q}}(n-1) \cup \mathrm{Cont}(q_n, f)$ is satisfiable
       and $\mathscr{SC}_{\mathcal{PC},\mathbf{q}}(n-1) \cup \mathrm{Cont}(q_n, f) \vDash \blacksquare\sigma$ for a $\sigma \in \mathcal{F_{SK}}$ **then**
15:     $a_n \leftarrow f$
16:   **else**
17:     $a_n \leftarrow u$
18:   **end if**
19:   $\mathscr{SC}_{\mathcal{PC},\mathbf{q}}(n) \leftarrow \mathscr{SC}_{\mathcal{PC},\mathbf{q}}(n-1) \cup \mathrm{Cont}(q_n, a_n)$
20: **end for**
21: **return a**

Concerning the last step, it follows from the first two steps, that both $\mathscr{H}_{\mathcal{PC},\mathbf{q}}(n-1)\cup\{\Diamond q_n\}$ and $\mathscr{H}_{\mathcal{PC},\mathbf{q}}(n-1)\cup\{\Diamond\neg q_n\}$ must be satisfiable. Hence by corollary 5.1.9 we conclude that $\mathscr{H}_{\mathcal{PC},\mathbf{q}}(n-1)\cup\mathrm{Cont}(q_n,u)$ is satisfiable. ∎

Lemma 5.3.11

The censor leRLCens *is not effective.* □

PROOF Consider the privacy configuration $\mathcal{PC}$ given by

$$\mathcal{QK} := \mathcal{AK} := (\emptyset, \emptyset) \text{ and } \mathcal{SK} := (\{\sigma\}, \emptyset).$$

In this case the query sequence $(\sigma, \sigma, \ldots)$ yields $(t, t, \ldots)$ and hence leads to the privacy violation $\mathscr{H}_{\mathcal{PC},\mathbf{q}}(1) \vDash \Box\sigma$. ∎

As a matter of fact, the discussed censor is massively ineffective. It will imply or even confirm a secret whenever it gets a chance without risking its credibility. An option to become "even more" ineffective would be to narrow into a secret, e.g. if a sub-query would be $(\ldots, \psi_1 \wedge \cdots \wedge \psi_n \rightarrow \sigma, \psi_1, \ldots \psi_n \ldots)$ the censor should answer t to ψ_1 to ψ_n (if possible), which is not necessarily done by the presented censor. But this would involve a structured analysis of the queried formulae, a feature that we -so far- do not want to equip our censors with. Additionally continuity would have to be dropped.

Lemma 5.3.12 (Repudiation)

The censor leRLCens *is repudiating.* □

PROOF Let $\mathcal{PC} = (\mathcal{QK}, \mathcal{AK}, \mathcal{SK})$ be a privacy configuration and $\mathbf{q}$ be a query-sequence. By construction of the algorithm it is clear that the given answers only depend on $\mathcal{AK}$ and not -by any means- on the actual database.

Hence $\mathcal{RK}_i := \mathcal{AK}$ is a possible choice as such a sequence.

As remarked, R-A) is immediate.

For R-B) notice, that –by definition of $\mathcal{PC}$– $\mathcal{AK}$ does not validate any secret.

From $\mathcal{AK} \vDash \mathcal{AK}$ also follows, that $(\mathcal{AK}, \mathcal{AK}, \mathcal{SK})$ is indeed a privacy-configuration and hence R-C), which completes the proof. ∎

Let us remark, that the presented censor is only interesting as an example to separate effectiveness and repudiation. A somehow reasonable censor should at least release sometimes "new" information (i.e. not known by the attacker yet) from the protected knowledge-base. In the above setting, the attacker only can learn the potential secrets in case it did not know them already. The censor is also extremely far from being minimally invasive.

Chapter 6

Conclusion

In this thesis we presented high quality censors against a singular attacker that achieve the presented privacy goals. For this purpose we established two levels of quality properties:

On a first level we formalized quality properties that are based on the belief presented by the censor, namely

credibility: the presented view is always consistent

effectiveness: all hidden secrets are not directly inferable from the presented view

On a second level, we discussed properties restricting the censor based on its answer selection methodology:

continuity: answer selection only depends on previously given answers

Truthful/Lying: whether the censor is restricted to true statements, or is allowed to lie

Cooperation a censor should always give an answer that matches the possible evaluation of a query (forcing a censor to lie)

Minimal Invasion: the censor should only distort an answer when answering the actual evaluation violates either credibility or effectiveness

Repudiation there should always be a database that does not violate any secret, but protected by the same censor would produce the exactly same answers

It was shown, that it is impossible for a truthful censor to have simultaneously all such properties. However, maximal truthful censors were presented:

RTCens being credible, effective, continuous and repudiating, but not minimal invasive

TCens being credible, effective, continuous and minimal invasive, but not repudiating

On the other hand, lying censors turned out to be optimal in that respect. Indeed they can have all desired properties. To this end, the—in this respect—best censor was constructed:

MILCens being credible, effective, continuous, minimal invasive and repudiating

All of them are however restricted to so called privacy configurations, that is start-situations in which the censor has access to the

104

full pre-knowledge of the attacker and the attacker does not know any secret at the start.

Index

Bibliography

[BB04a] BISKUP, Joachim ; BONATTI, Piero A.: Controlled query evaluation for enforcing confidentiality in complete information systems. In: *Int. J. Inf. Sec.* 3 (2004), Nr. 1, S. 14–27. http://dx.doi.org/10.1007/s10207-004-0032-1. – DOI 10.1007/s10207–004–0032–1

[BB04b] BISKUP, Joachim ; BONATTI, Piero A.: Controlled Query Evaluation for Known Policies by Combining Lying and Refusal. In: *Ann. Math. Artif. Intell.* 40 (2004), Nr. 1-2, S. 37–62

[BB07] BISKUP, Joachim ; BONATTI, Piero A.: Controlled query evaluation with open queries for a decidable relational submodel. In: *Annals of Mathematics and Artificial Intelligence* 50 (2007), Nr. 1-2, S. 39–77. http://dx.doi.org/10.1007/s10472-007-9070-5. – DOI 10.1007/s10472–007–9070–5. – ISSN 1012–2443

[BBG+63] BACKUS, J. W. ; BAUER, F. L. ; GREEN, J. ; KATZ,
C. ; MCCARTHY, J. ; PERLIS, A. J. ; RUTISHAUSER,
H. ; SAMELSON, K. ; VAUQUOIS, B. ; WEGSTEIN,
J. H. ; WIJNGAARDEN, A. van ; WOODGER, M.: Re-
vised Report on the Algorithm Language ALGOL 60.
In: *Commun. ACM* 6 (1963), Januar, Nr. 1, S. 1–17.
http://dx.doi.org/10.1145/366193.366201. – DOI
10.1145/366193.366201. – ISSN 0001–0782

[BCM+03] BAADER, Franz (Hrsg.) ; CALVANESE, Diego (Hrsg.)
; MCGUINNESS, Deborah L. (Hrsg.) ; NARDI, Daniele
(Hrsg.) ; PATEL-SCHNEIDER, Peter F. (Hrsg.): *The description logic handbook: theory, implementation, and
applications*. New York, NY, USA : Cambridge Univer-
sity Press, 2003. – ISBN 0–521–78176–0

[Bis00] BISKUP, Joachim: For unknown secrecies refusal is
better than lying. In: *Data & Knowledge Engineering* 33 (2000), Nr. 1, 1-23. http://dx.doi.org/10.
1016/S0169-023X(99)00043-9. – DOI 10.1016/S0169–
023X(99)00043–9. – ISSN 0169–023X

[BKS95] BONATTI, Piero A. ; KRAUS, Sarit ; SUBRAHMANIAN,
V. s.: Foundations of Secure Deductive Databases.
In: *Transactions on Knowledge and Data Engineering*
7 (1995), Nr. 3, S. 406–422. http://dx.doi.org/10.
1109/69.390247. – DOI 10.1109/69.390247. – ISSN
1041–4347

BIBLIOGRAPHY

[BW08]   BISKUP, Joachim ; WEIBERT, Torben: Keeping secrets
in incomplete databases. In: *Int. J. Inf. Secur.* 7 (2008),
Mai, Nr. 3, S. 199–217. http://dx.doi.org/10.1007/
s10207-007-0037-7. – DOI 10.1007/s10207–007–0037–
7. – ISSN 1615–5262

[Sch08]   SCHÖNING, U.:   *Theoretische Informatik - kurz
gefasst.* Spektrum Akademischer Verlag, 2008 (Spektrum
Hochschultaschenbücher). – ISBN 9783827418241

[SDJR83]   SICHERMAN, George L. ; DE JONGE, Wiebren ; RIET,
Reind P. d.: Answering queries without revealing secrets.
In: *ACM Trans. Database Syst.* 8 (1983), Nr. 1, S. 41–59.
http://dx.doi.org/10.1145/319830.319833. – DOI
10.1145/319830.319833. – ISSN 0362–5915

[SS05]   STOFFEL, Kilian ; STUDER, Thomas: Provable Data
Privacy. In: VIBORG, K. (Hrsg.) ; DEBENHAM, J. (Hrsg.)
; WAGNER, R. (Hrsg.): *DEXA 2005* Bd. 3588, Springer,
2005 (LNCS), S. 324–332

[SS07]   STOUPPA, Phiniki ; STUDER, Thomas: A formal model
of data privacy. In: VIRBITSKAITE, Irina (Hrsg.) ;
VORONKOV, Andrei (Hrsg.) ; Springer (Veranst.): *Pro-
ceedings of Perspectives of System Informatics* Bd. 4378
Springer, Springer, 2007, 401-411

[SS09]   STOUPPA, Phiniki ; STUDER, Thomas: Data Privacy
for *ALC* Knowledge Bases. In: ARTEMOV, S. (Hrsg.) ;
NERODE, A. (Hrsg.): *LFCS 2009* Bd. 5407, Springer,
2009 (LNCS), S. 409–421

[Stu13]   STUDER, Thomas: A Universal Approach to Guaran-
            tee Data Privacy. In: *Logica Universalis* 7 (2013), Nr.
            2, 195-209. http://www.iam.unibe.ch/ltgpub/2012/
            stu12b.pdf

[SW14]   STUDER, Thomas ; WERNER, Johannes: Censors
            for Boolean Description Logic.   In: *Transactions on
            Data Privacy* 7 (2014), 223-252. http://www.tdp.cat/
            issues11/abs.a138a13.php. – ISSN 1888–5063

ERKLÄRUNG

gemäss Art. 28 Abs 2 RSL 05

Name/Vorname: Werner Johannes

Matrikelnummer: 11-104-429

Studiengang: Doktorand

Bachelor ☐   Master ☐   Dissertation ☒

Titel der Arbeit: Controlled Query Evaluation
in General Semantics
with Incomplete Information

Leiter der Arbeit: Prof. Dr. T. Studer

Ich erkläre hiermit, dass ich diese Arbeit selbstständig verfasst und keine anderen als die angegebenen Quellen benutzt habe. Alle Stellen, die wörtlich oder sinngemäss aus Quellen entnommen wurden, habe ich als solche gekennzeichnet. Mir ist bekannt, dass andernfalls der Senat gemäss Artikel 36 Absatz 1 Buchstabe r des Gesetzes vom 5. September 1996 über die Universität zum Entzug des auf Grund dieser Arbeit verliehenen Titels berechtigt ist.

Bern, den 23. April 2015

Ort/Datum

_____

Unterschrift

LEBENSLAUF

1983   Geboren am 30. Juli in Erlangen

1989-1993   Loschge-Grundschule Erlangen

1993-2002   Christian-Ernst-Gymnasium Erlangen

2002-2008   Diplomstudiengang Informatik an der Friedrich-Alexander-Universität Erlangen-Nürnberg mit Schwerpunktfach: Theoretische Informatik

2004-2009   Diplomstudiengang Mathematik an der Friedrich-Alexander-Universität Erlangen-Nürnberg mit Schwerpunktfach: Darstellungstheorie

2009-2011   Wissenschaftlicher Mitarbeiter am Department Informatik *Lehrstuhl 10 - Systemsimulation* der Friedrich-Alexander-Universität Erlangen-Nürnberg

2011-2015   Doktorand bei Prof. Dr. Studer an der Universität Bern, Forschungsgruppe *Logic and Theory Group*

www.ingramcontent.com/pod-product-compliance
Lightning Source LLC
Chambersburg PA
CBHW071222050326
40689CB00011B/2419